DATE DUE

OCT 16 1995	
DEC 15 2008	
MAY 08 2012	
OCT 24 2019	

Modern Critical Views

T.S. ELIOT

Edited with an introduction by

Harold Bloom

Sterling Professor of the Humanities
Yale University

1985
CHELSEA HOUSE PUBLISHERS
New York

PROJECT EDITORS: Emily Bestler, James Uebbing
EDITORIAL COORDINATOR: Karyn Browne
EDITORIAL STAFF: Joy Johannessen, Sally Stepanek, Linda Grossman
RESEARCH: Kevin Pask
DESIGN: Susan Lusk

Cover illustration by Kye Carbone
Composition provided by Collage Publications, Inc., New York

Printed and bound in the United States of America

Library of Congress Cataloging in Publication Data
T.S. Eliot, modern critical views.
    Bibliography: p.
    Contents: Introduction/Harold Bloom—
Ash-Wednesday/Hugh Kenner—Antique drum/Northrup Frye—[etc.]
    1. Eliot, T.S. (Thomas Stearns), 1888–1965—Criticism
and interpretation—Addresses, essays, lectures.
I. Bloom, Harold.
PS3509.L43Z8726   1984   821'.912   84-22930
ISBN 0–87754–601–0

Chelsea House Publishers
Harold Steinberg, Chairman & Publisher
Susan Lusk, Vice President
A Division of Chelsea House Educational Communications, Inc.
133 Christopher Street, New York, NY 10014

Contents

Introduction

I

Thomas Stearns Eliot is a central figure in the Western literary culture of this century. His undoubted achievement as a lyric and elegiac poet in itself would suffice to establish him in the main Romantic tradition of British and American poetry that moves from Wordsworth and Whitman on to Geoffrey Hill and John Ashbery, poets of our moment. There is an obvious irony in such a judgment. Eliot's professed sense of *the* tradition, *his* tradition, was rather different, tracing as it did the true line of poetry in English from its origins in medieval Provence and Italy through its later developments in France. I borrow that remark from Northrop Frye, whose sympathetic but dissenting analysis of Eliot's cultural polemic is reprinted in this collection. Eliot's polemical stance as a literary critic can be distinguished from his rhetorical stance as a poet, and both postures of the spirit are fortunately quite distinct from his cultural position, self-proclaimed as Anglo-Catholic, Royalist and Classical.

An obsessive reader of poetry growing up in the nineteen thirties and forties entered a critical world dominated by the opinions and example of Eliot. To speak out of even narrower personal experience, anyone adopting the profession of teaching literature in the early nineteen fifties entered a discipline virtually enslaved not only by Eliot's insights but by the entire span of his preferences and prejudices. If one's cultural position was Jewish, Liberal and Romantic, one was likely to start out with a certain lack of affection for Eliot's predominance, however much (against the will) the subtle force of the poetry was felt. If a young critic particularly loved Shelley, Milton, Emerson, Pater, and if that same critic did not believe that Blake was a naive and eccentric genius, then regard for Eliot seemed unnecessary. Whatever he actually represented, a neochristian and neoclassic Academy had exalted him, by merit raised, to what was pragmatically rather a bad eminence. In *that* critical climate, Hopkins was considered the only valid Victorian poet, greatly superior to Browning and Tennyson, while Whitman seemed an American nightmare and Wallace Stevens, if he passed at all, had to be salvaged as a Late Augustan. Thirty years on, these views have a kind of antique charm, but in 1954 they were at least annoying, and if one cared enough, they had some capacity for infuriating.

I resume these matters not to stir up waning rancors, but to explain why, for some critics of my own generation, Eliot only recently has ceased to represent the spiritual enemy. His disdain for Freud, his flair for demonstrating the authenticity of his Christianity by exhibiting a judicious anti-Semitism, his refined contempt for human sexuality—somehow these did not seem to be the inevitable foundations for contemporary culture. Granted that he refrained from the rhetorical excesses of his ally Ezra Pound; there is nothing in him resembling the Poundian apothegm: "All the jew part of the Bible is black evil." Still, an Academy that found its ideology in Eliot was not a place where one could teach comfortably, or where one could have remained, had the Age of Eliot not begun to wane. The ascendency of Eliot, as a fact of cultural politics, is something many among us could not wish to see return.

II

Eliot asserted for his poetry a seventeenth century ancestry, out of Jacobean dramatists and Metaphysical lyricists. Its actual forerunners are Whitman and Tennyson, and Eliot's strength is felt now when we read "When Lilacs Last in the Dooryard Bloom'd" and "Maud: A Monodrama," and find ourselves believing that they are influenced by The Waste Land. It is a neglected truth of American poetic history that Eliot and Stevens are more Whitmanian than Hart Crane, whose allegiance to Whitman was overt. Though Eliot and Stevens consciously did not feel or know it, their poetry is obsessed with Whitman's poetry. By this I mean Whitman's tropes and Whitman's curious transitions between topics, and not at all the example of Whitman, far more crucial for Crane and many others.

It is the pattern of Eliot's figurations that is most High Romantic, a pattern that I suspect he learned from Tennyson and Whitman, who derived it from Keats and Shelley, who in turn had been instructed by Wordsworth's crisis lyrics and odes, which go back yet further to Spenserian and Miltonic models. Consider Eliot's "Ash-Wednesday," his conversion-sequence of 1930. The poem's six movements are not a Dantesque Vita Nuova, despite Eliot's desires, but a rather strict re-enactment of the Wordsworthian drama of experiential loss and compensatory imaginative gain:

(I) This is an ironic movement that says "I rejoice" but means "I despair," which is the limited irony that Freud terms a "reaction formation," or an emotion masking ambivalently as its opposite. Despite the deliberate allusions to Cavalcanti and Dante, Ezekiel and the Mass, that throng the poem, the presumably unintended echoes of Wordsworth's "Intimations of

Immortality" Ode carry the reader closer to the center of the poet's partially repressed anxieties and to his poetic anxieties in particular. "The infirm glory" and the "one veritable transitory power" are stigmata of the visionary gleam in its flight from the poet, and if what is lost here is more-than-natural, we remember that the loss in Wordsworth also transcends nature. Though Eliot employs the language of mysticism and Wordsworth the language of nature, the crisis for each is poetic rather than mystical or natural. Eliot's renunciation of voice, however ironical, leads directly to what for many readers has been the most memorable and poignant realization in the sequence: "Consequently I rejoice, having to construct something / Upon which to rejoice." No more illuminating epigraph could be assigned to Wordsworth's "Intimations" Ode, or to "Tintern Abbey" or "Resolution and Independence." The absence lamented in the first part of "Ash Wednesday" is a once-present poetic strength, whatever else it represented experientially. In the Shakespearean rejection of the desire for "this man's gift and that man's scope," we need not doubt that the men are precursor poets, nor ought we to forget that not hoping to turn again is also an ironic farewell to troping, and so to one's own quest for poetic voice.

(II) The question that haunts the transition between the first two sections, pragmatically considered, is: "Am I, Eliot, still a poet?" "Shall these bones live?" is a synecdochal question, whole for part, since the immortality involved is the figurative survival of one's poetry: "As I am forgotten / And would be forgotten, so I would forget." Turning around against himself, this poet, in the mode of Browning's Childe Roland, asks only to be numbered among the scattered precursors, to fail as they have failed: "We have our inheritance."

(III) After such self-wounding, the poet seeks a kind of Pauline *kenosis*, akin to Christ's emptying himself of his own Divinity, which here can only mean the undoing of one's poetic gift. As inspiration fades away willfully, the gift wonderfully declares itself nevertheless, in that enchanted lyricism Eliot never ceased to share with the elegiac Whitman and the Virgilian Tennyson: "Lilac and brown hair; / Distraction, music of the flute, stops and steps of the mind over the third stair." The figurative movement is metonymic, as in the displacement of poetic power from the speaker to the curiously Pre-Raphaelite "broadbacked figure drest in blue and green," who is anything but a possible representation of Eliot's own poetic self.

(IV) This is the daemonic vision proper, allowing a sequence that denies sublimity, to re-attain a Romantic Sublime. In the transition between sections III and IV, Eliot appears to surmount the temptations of solipsism, so as to ask and answer the question: "Am I capable of loving another?" The unnamed other or "silent sister" is akin to shadowy images of desire in

Tennyson and Whitman, narcissistic emblems certainly, but pointing beyond the self's passion for the self. Hugh Kenner, indubitably Eliot's best and most Eliotic critic, suggestively compares "Ash Wednesday" to Tennyson's "The Holy Grail," and particulary to the fearful death-march of Percivale's quest in that most ornate portion of *The Idylls of the King.* Kenner of course awards the palm to Eliot over what he dismisses as a crude "Victorian ceremony of iterations" as compared to Eliot's "austere gestures of withdrawal and submission." A quarter of a century after he made them, Kenner's judgments seem eminently reversible, since Tennyson's gestures are, in this case, palpably more austere than his inheritor's. Tennyson has, after all, nothing quite so gaudy as: "Redeem / The unread vision in the higher dream / While jewelled unicorns draw by the guilded hearse."

(V) Percivale's desert, and the wasteland of Browning's Childe Roland, join the Biblical wildernesses in this extraordinary *askesis*, a self-curtailing rhapsody that truncates Romantic tradition as much as it does Eliot's individual talent. One could assert that this section affirms all the possibilities of sublimation, from Plato through Nietzsche to Freud, except that the inside/outside metaphor of dualism confines itself here only to "The Word without a word, the Word within." Eliot, like all his Romantic ancestors from Wordsworth to Pater, seeks a crossing to a subtle identification with an innocent earliness, while fearing to introject instead the belatedness of a world without imagination, the death-in-life of the poet who has outlasted his gift.

(VI) This is one of Eliot's triumphs, as an earliness is recovered under the sign of contrition. The "unbroken wings" still flying seaward are a beautiful metalepsis of the wings of section I, which were "merely vans to beat the air." A characteristic pattern of the Romantic crisis lyric is extended as the precursors return from the dead, but in Eliot's own colors, the "lost lilac" of Whitman and the "lost sea voices" of Tennyson joining Eliot's "lost heart" in the labor of rejoicing, having indeed constructed something upon which to rejoice.

III

Eliot is hardly unique among the poets in having misrepresented either his actual tradition or his involuntary place in that tradition. His cultural influence, rather than his polemic, was closer to being an unique phenomenon. To have been born in 1888, and to have died in 1965, is to have flourished in the Age of Freud, hardly a time when Anglo-Catholic theology, social thought, and morality were central to the main movement of mind.

Even a few sentences of Eliotic polemic, chosen at random, seem unreal in the world of 1984:

> It would perhaps be more natural, as well as in better conformity with the Will of God, if there were more celibates and if those who were married had larger families...
>
> If you will not have God (and He is a jealous God) you should pay your respects to Hitler or Stalin.
>
> ...a positive culture must have a positive set of values, and the dissentients must remain marginal, tending to make only marginal contributions.

These are excerpts from *The Idea of a Christian Society* and were written in 1939. Frank Kermode, a distinguished authority on Eliot, writing in 1975, insisted "that Eliot profoundly changed our thinking about poetry and criticism without trying to impose as a condition of his gift the acceptance of consequences which, for him, followed as a matter of reason, as well as of belief and personal vocation." It may well be that the largest difference between Kermode's critical generation, in England, and the next generation, in America, is that we changed our thinking about poetry and criticism in reaction against Eliot's thinking, precisely because Eliot's followers had imposed upon us consequences peculiar to his belief and his personal vocation. Whether Eliot's discriminations were so fine as Kermode asserts is yet another matter. Shelley's skeptical yet passionate beliefs, according to Eliot, were not coherent, not mature, not founded upon the facts of experience. Eliot once gave thanks that Walter Pater never wrote about *Hamlet*; would that Eliot never had done so. We would have been spared the influential but unfortunate judgment "that here Shakespeare tackled a problem which proved too much for him." Eliot doubtless is in the line of poet-critics: Ben Jonson, Dryden, Dr. Samuel Johnson, Coleridge, Poe and Arnold are among those who precede him. As a critic, he does not approach the first four, but surely equals Poe and Arnold, equivocal praise, though he certainly surpassed Poe and Arnold as poets. It is difficult to prophesy that Eliot's criticism will prove to be of permanent value, but perhaps we need to await the arrival of a generation neither formed by him nor rebelling against him, before we justly can place him.

IV

That Eliot, in retrospect, will seem the Matthew Arnold rather than the Abraham Cowley of his age, is the sympathetic judgment of A. Walton Litz.

For motives admitted already, one might prefer to see Eliot as the Cowley, and some celebrated passages in *Four Quartets* are worthy of comparison with long-ago-admired Pindarics of that forgotten wit, but Arnold's burden as involuntary belated Romantic is indeed close to Eliot's. A direct comparison of Eliot's elegiac achievement to Whitman's or Tennyson's seems to me both more problematical and more inevitable. "Gerontion" contrasts unfavorably to "Tithonus" or "Ulysses," while *The Waste Land*, despite its critical high priests, lacks the coherence, maturity and experiential authenticity of "When Lilacs Last in the Dooryard Bloom'd." And yet it must be admitted that Eliot is what the closing lines of *The Waste Land* assert him to be: a shorer of fragments against his (and our) ruins. The phantasmagoric intensity of his best poems and passages can be matched only in the greatest visionaries and poets of Western literature. It is another paradox that the Anglo-Catholic, Royalist, Classical spokesperson should excel in the mode of fictive hallucination and lyric derangement, in the fashioning of nightmare images perfectly expressive of his age.

Eliot's influence as a poet is by no means spent, yet it seems likely that Robert Penn Warren's later poetry, the most distinguished now being written among us, will be the final stand of Eliot's extraordinary effort to establish an anti-Romantic counter-Sublime sense of *the* tradition to replace the continuity of Romantic tradition. That the continuity now has absorbed him is hardly a defeat; absorption is not rejection, and Eliot's poetry is securely in the canon. Eliot's strength, manifested in the many poets indebted to him, is probably most authentically commemorated by the poetry of Hart Crane, which engages Eliot's poetry in an agon without which Crane could not have achieved his difficult greatness. One can prefer Crane to Eliot, as I do, and yet be forced to concede that Eliot, more than Whitman, made Crane possible.

V

The essays in this collection chronicle the agon that criticism has entered into with Eliot, primarily with Eliot's major poems. I have arranged them in the order of their publication, with only the first two, by Kenner and Frye, representing the literary climate while Eliot was still alive. Kenner, then and now, is Eliot's champion, to the extent of apparently preferring Eliot's verse dramas to Shakespeare's:

> None of the actors, deprived of fine lines to mouth, is allowed to affirm a vision centered on himself, as Othello does, as Hamlet does. And if they are deprived of that satisfaction, it is because the plays are about privacy, not affirmation. Shakespeare's is for better or worse a universe of actors, strut-

ting and fretting; and so is the universe of *The Waste Land*; but the universe of Eliot's dramatic comedies is a universe of persons who learn to discard the satisfactions of the imprisoning role.

That is Kenner in 1962; reading him again after more than twenty years is to learn that "modernism" is only another defensive antiquarianism. Northrop Frye, a year later, began the Romantic counter-offensive by noting that Eliot rather disapproved of Shakespeare because "Shakespeare does not always take a maturely dim view of human nature." The remaining critics in this volume wrote during the 1970's and the early 1980's, and are none of them Eliotics, like Kenner or such allied figures as F.R. Leavis, R.P. Blackmur, and Cleanth Brooks, all of whom placed Eliot with the sages as well as with the poets. But the critics whom I reprint here are, like Frye, in a more benign relation to Eliot than I can achieve. Olney, Goldman, Donoghue, Ellmann, Gordon, Nevo and Jay do not read Eliot as a cultural prophet or as a secular saint. They study him, with sympathy and insight, as one of the representative poets of his time, and each of them adds to our increasingly accurate sense of his authentic relation to poetic history.

Eliot, writing in 1948, ended his *Notes Towards the Definition of Culture* by affirming that the culture of Europe could not survive the disappearance of the Christian faith, because: "It is in Christianity that our arts have developed... It is against a background of Christianity that all our thought has significance." That seems to be the center of Eliot's polemic, and each reader must make of it what she or he can or will. The Age of Freud, Kafka and Proust, of Yeats, Wallace Stevens, Beckett: somehow these thoughts and visions suggest a very different definition of culture than the Eliotic one. Perhaps it was fortunate for Eliot that he was a Late Romantic poet long before he became, for a time, the cultural oracle of the academies.

HUGH KENNER

Ash-Wednesday

*What then, shall I continually 'fall' and never 'rise'? 'turn away' and not
once 'turn again'? Shall my rebellions be 'perpetual'?*

—LANCELOT ANDREWES

*. . . a beautiful and ineffectual angel, beating in the void his luminous wings
in vain.*

—MATTHEW ARNOLD

A thin, firm minor music, of cere-
monious intricacy, dissolving the world of Tiresias, Hamlet, and Mrs. Equi-
tone, creating in the zone vacated by that world "a place of solitude where
three dreams cross"; a visionary precision in which a symbolic stair has
(incidentally) a banister, and three symbolic leopards sit quietly because their
stomachs are full; a wholly transparent network of allusions, tacitly
nourished, like a nervous system, from secret sources among which research
will discover nothing irrelevant; a religious poem which contains no slovenly
phrase, no borrowed zeal, no formulated piety: this improbable achievement
subsumes for good the secular Eliot whose traces of Original Richard Savage
precipitated in his poems an arresting residue of gritty substantiality. We are
to hear no more of how

> Apeneck Sweeney spreads his knees
> Letting his arms hang down to laugh,

nor will such a detail as "rats' feet over broken glass" momentarily usurp the world.

> And a time for the wind to break the loosened pane
> And to shake the wainscot where the field-mouse trots,
> And to shake the tattered arras woven with a silent motto.

In these lines from *East Coker* we see images from one of Eliot's familiar constellations functioning in a new way. The trotting field-mouse is a figure in a poemscape, not like the rat in *The Hollow Men* the synecdoche of some omnipresent world. The most arresting images now *recede*; intensity inheres in the design of the whole passage, not in the immutable phrase. His former idiom had tended toward opacity. Its savor lay in the gestures of real speech exactly caught. The vice that menaced it was a certain succinct impenetrability ("this broken jaw of our lost kingdoms"). The language after *Ash-Wednesday* is characteristically open, even tranquil, its aim a ritual translucency, its lapses into facility and small talk. Some withdrawal from individual speech has occurred, which resembles a loss of vigor, though the vigor is rather dispersed than evaporated. This poetry is related less intimately now to the speaking voice than to renovated decorums of the impersonal English language. Its substance even becomes to some extent its own decorousness

> -every phrase
> And sentence that is right (where every word is at home,
> Taking its place to support the others, . . .
> The common word exact without vulgarity,
> The formal word precise but not pedantic,
> The complete consort dancing together),
> Every phrase and every sentence is an end and a beginning,
> Every poem an epitaph.

This points to the animating principle of *Ash-Wednesday*, its own autonomous virtuosity in a universe implying adjacent spiritual states, but wholly compounded of verbal suggestions. From node to node of its own structure, from zone to zone, the poem moves swiftly like a swallow, and without flutter. Arrived in each zone, it circles and searches before passing on, making its way in this fashion from the zone of feeling dominated by "Because . . ." to the domain of "although . . . ," from a ratiocinative submission ("Because I know . . ." "Consequently I rejoice . . .") in the place where "there is nothing again," to a tension among substantial presences ("And the weak spirit quickens to rebel / For the bent golden-rod and the lost sea smell") that has no use for "because" and "consequently."

What is achieved—we are driven to impersonal summary—is a tension: more than the Magus achieved. He arrived at a disenchantment which "another death" might make right. Sweeney too lost the taste for created things. The center of perception that moves through *Ash-Wednesday* (a focal point as specific as an "I" can be, but too wholly absorbed in its own spiritual states to be called a protagonist:), the "I," the Voice, the "finite center," begins where the Magus left off, and moves on: not at the last merely "no longer at ease here, in the old dispensation," but installed in a realm of superior wakefulness where

> . . . the lost heart stiffens and rejoices
> In the lost lilac and the lost sea voices
> And the weak spirit quickens to rebel
> For the bent golden-rod and the lost sea smell
> Quickens to recover
> The cry of quail and the whirling plover
> And the blind eye creates
> The empty forms between the ivory gates
> And smell renews the salt savour of the sandy earth.

Here every noun, verb and adjective pulls two ways. The heart is lost to the world and lost in the world. It stiffens with life and with rebellion. The lilac is lost in belonging to the world that has been renounced, and the heart "rejoices" either to applaud its departure or to bring it back transfigured: this last a thin possibility inhering only in the overtone emphatic placement confers upon "rejoices," a possibility so nearly illusory that the phrase "weak spirit" remains appropriate in its presence. The senses, by the same implication of transfiguration and recovery, renew "the salt savour of the sandy earth"; but the parallel with the delusions created by the "blind eye" and the doubtful force of "sandy" (Is it really fruitful earth? What are its relations with "the desert in the garden" of Part V and with the desert of "the blessing of sand" in Part II?) increase the tension of implicit delusion. From which follows—

> Suffer us not to mock ourselves with falsehood
> Teach us to care and not to care
> Teach us to sit still
> And even among these rocks
> Our peace in His will
> And even among these rocks
> Sister, mother
> And spirit of the river, spirit of the sea,
> Suffer me not to be separated
> And let my cry come unto Thee.

"Teach us to care and not to care." The tension itself is a good. This line and its companion have not the context of resignation that sponsored their first appearance in Part I; or rather, the resignation is of greater purity. The ambivalent "separated" rejects internal separation as well as separation from

God. Without specifying what evades specification, it is permissible for commentary to suggest that the opposite pull of the senses and the devotional spirit—of God's creation and God—is to be maintained as a fruitful and essential equivocalness, not "solved" by relegating one half of the being to the earth and the other half to heaven, nor yet, as in the Buddhist Fire Sermon, by becoming "weary of the knowledge of the visible" and so "empty of desire." A temptation to deny the senses must be resisted, rather as Becket in *Murder in the Cathedral* contends with the temptation to appoint himself martyr.

That is where the poem goes. It arrives there by a climbing of stairs, a vision, and a vertigo of assonances where

>. . . the unstilled world still whirled
>About the centre of the silent Word.

Before the stairs, it undergoes a dismemberment of all corporeality, by three white leopards; over this scene of macabre tranquillity presides the goodness of a Lady who subsequently withdraws herself

>In a white gown, to contemplation, in a white gown.

The composition of this strange scene includes a juniper tree, bones, and a desert, dreamily static like an invention of the Douanier Rousseau's. It is evidently the first phase of that which is constructed "upon which to rejoice," according to the proposal in the first section of all:

>Because I cannot hope to turn again
>Consequently I rejoice, having to construct something
>Upon which to rejoice
>
>And pray to God to have mercy upon us
>And I pray that I may forget
>These matters that with myself I too much discuss
>Too much explain

The middle sections of the poem, consequently, neither discuss nor explain, but pursue that "logic of the imagination" for which in his Introduction to Perse's *Anabase* Eliot in 1930 claimed a status coequal with that of the familiar logic of concepts. The first part, however, allies itself to that zone of consciousness where discussion is carried on, and with the aid of a form which suggests a strict form in echoing the melodic freedom of the Cavalcanti *ballate*, it adapts the ceremonious wraith of a syllogism to the uses of an ideal self-examination.

>Because I do not hope to turn again
>Because I do not hope
>Because I do not hope to turn
>Desiring this man's gift and that man's scope

> I no longer strive to strive towards such things
> (Why should the agèd eagle stretch its wings?)
> Why should I mourn
> The vanished power of the usual reign?

"Perch'io non spero di tornar gia mai . . ." so Guido Cavalcanti expecting to die in exile commences the dialogue with the Ballata he is sending to his distant lady: the dialogue with the Ballata is the Ballata itself, much as Eliot's resolve to construct something upon which to rejoice is itself an element in the construction.

> Because no hope is left me, Ballatetta,
> Of return to Tuscany,
> Light-foot go thou some fleet way
> Unto my Lady straightway,
> And out of her courtesy
> Great honour will she do thee.

With Cavalcanti's plight is associated the mood of Shakespeare, one of his hundred moods:

> When in disgrace with fortune and men's eyes,
> I all alone beweep my outcast state
> And trouble deaf heaven with my bootless cries,
> And look upon myself and curse my fate:
> Wishing me like to one more rich in hope,
> Featured like him, like him with friends possessed,
> Desiring this man's art and that man's scope . . .

This English Renaissance fit of the sulks, readily cured by thinking of something else ("haply I think on thee . . ."), is transcended by Cavalcanti's irremediable plight just as Cavalcanti's is transcended by the metaphysical despair of Ash-Wednesday, when the Christian universe examines its own unworthiness. The *Ash-Wednesday* language bears a similar relation to Shakespeare's: it is emptied of irrelevant specificity: the speaker does not quaintly "trouble deaf heaven" but moves as if through the phases of some liturgy, in an unpunctuated *stil nuovo*, cadenced rather than counted, pre-Elizabethan, not mediaeval, a language never spoken anywhere, though never remote in its deliberate bare elegance from the constructions (if not the energies) of actual speech. Though the cadences swing with the untrammeled gravity of a Foucault pendulum, the idiom is devoid of copiousness: when we come upon "the infirm glory of the positive hour" we are aware of "infirm" and "positive," two deliberate words, neither one resonant, each salient in the grave nerveless ambience. So with "the one veritable transitory power": these rare polysyllables bring with them an air of exactness without momentum. The energy of the line has precisely expended itself in establishing two precise words, and there is none left over to propel the next line to some rhetorical pitch. The next line is simply, "Because I cannot drink."

The other dimension of the opening is an insistent mellifluousness, nearly Tennysonian, located in the long vowels and associating itself with the recurrent pairings of identical words ("I no longer strive to strive towards such things"; "Because I know I shall not know") and with the liturgical repetition of constructions, phrases, and whole lines. It is this quality that sets the language of *Ash-Wednesday* at a remove from speech, so much so that we are driven for analogy as far as the Laureate's *Holy Grail*:

> Then every evil word I had spoken once,
> And every evil thought I had thought of old,
> And every evil deed I ever did,
> Awoke and cried, "This Quest is not for thee."
> And lifting up mine eyes, I found myself
> Alone, and in a land of sand and thorns,
> And I was thirsty, even unto death;
> And I too cried, "This Quest is not for thee."

The Victorian ceremony of iterations is crude beside Eliot's austere gestures of withdrawal and submission; nevertheless, it appears to have been under his eye. A few lines later Sir Percivale is telling of the delusions that beset him on his quest; he came to a brook with apple trees.

> But even while I drank the brook, and ate
> The goodly apples, all these things at once
> Fell into dust and I was left alone
> And thirsting in a land of sand and thorns.

which may be the source of

> Because I cannot drink
> There, where trees flower, and springs flow, for there is nothing again

Percivale proceeds to encounter what Eliot calls "the infirm glory of the positive hour," in the shape of a knight

> In golden armour with a crown of gold
> About a casque all jewels; and his horse
> In golden armour jewell'd everywhere;

he likewise fell into dust. Later in *The Holy Grail* Sir Lancelot climbs stairs towards a vision—

> up I climb'd a thousand steps
> With pain: as in a dream I seem'd to climb
> For ever;

the vision when he encounters it is veiled.

By way of Tennyson, *Ash-Wednesday* is united with certain *Waste*

Land themes: the quester, the Chapel Perilous, the elusive vision associated with a lady. By way of Dante, the lady, appearing on three planes, gathers divinity. In the desert she is withdrawn to contemplation, like the earthly Beatrice. In the vision that follows the scene on the stairs, she appears veiled in white and blue, capable of making strong the fountains and fresh the springs, functioning in the economy of the poem somewhat as Beatrice does in Canto XXX of the *Purgatorio*. Though she goes "in Mary's colour" she is not Mary; yet she is perhaps also "the veiled sister" of Part V, who may pray "for those who wait in darkness," and who in the finale of the poem is so closely associated with the "holy mother" as to be virtually identified with her.

When we first become aware of her, she is not, however, a wholly settling presence; there is even something a little sinister in the indifference of her withdrawal ("in a white gown, to contemplation, in a white gown") after the leopards have completed their feast. She is in more than one way a "Lady of silences," and if she is "Calm and distressed / Torn and most whole," those are qualities not only of supernatural compassion, but of natural derangement, proper to the sphere of the Hyacinth girl's unnerving simplicity, and to the fact that the positive hour's glory ("looking into the heart of Light, the silence") is "infirm." Not that these vaguely troubling implications are of any salience; the remote, cool ritual verse obliterates all but our most determined attention to the normal range of certain words. In Part II, with its "I who am here dissembled" and its willed forgetting, we inhabit a *protective* peace, dreamlike, just below the threshold of a less soothing wakefulness. Parts III and IV are not so fragile; the "devil of the stairs" and the "cloud of tears" do not menace a dream, they are components of a vision.

Plainly the speaker is in some unspecifiable way thrusting past experiences into the destructive element of symbol, though it is pointless to fuss about the poem's sequence of events, or to determine which of its scenes may be recollections, which presences. It is true that the verbs in Parts II, III and IV are chiefly in the past tense, but Eliot's tenses are frequently opportunisms, as in *Triumphal March*, for dimming or vivifying. Grammatically, five minutes ago is as much in the past as twenty years ago. In Part IV, however, we hear of "the years that walk between," and are at liberty to suppose that the lady who once enlivened the Waste Land, "made cool the dry rock and made firm the sand," did so on the far side of those years, in "the positive hour," perhaps, and that the injunction "Sovegna vos," if we are to press the parallel with Arnaut's speech in *Purgatorio*, Canto XXVI, is addressed to her out of a present metaphorical fire. For the years restore her:

> Here are the years that walk between, bearing
> Away the fiddles and the flutes, restoring
> One who moves in the time between sleep and waking, wearing

> White light folded, sheathed about her, folded,
> The new years walk, restoring
> Through a bright cloud of tears, the years, restoring
> With a new verse the ancient rhyme. . . .

The parallel with the iterated participles that introduce *The Waste Land* seems deliberate: on that occasion, a "covering" and an umbilical "feeding" that resist the Spring's breeding, mixing, and stirring; on this occasion, a welcoming of what the new years bring even as they seem to be taking gratifying things away. They restore "with a new verse, the ancient rhyme,' not only enhancing the present but bestowing meaning on the neutral past. As we are to be told in *The Dry Salvages*,

> approach to the meaning restores the experience
> In a different form, beyond any meaning
> We can assign to happiness.

The "white gown" of her faintly unsettling withdrawal in Part II is now "white light," as she moves in the time between sleep and waking. The function of her departure and restoration is somewhat explicated in *Marina*, an Ariel Poem published a few months after *Ash-Wednesday*. Here an epigraph from Seneca's *Hercules Furens* tugs against the explicit parallels with Shakespeare's *Pericles* sufficiently hard to arouse a slight but stubborn possibility that the speaker may be mocking himself with falsehood. The epigraph, spoken by a man who has slaughtered his children and is now recovering sanity, tends to align certain motifs of *Pericles* with the Eliotic sequence of perhaps-drowned women, though it is true that when Shakespeare's hero threw his queen into the sea he supposed her already dead. In the shipboard scene (V:i) in which the king's lost daughter is restored to him as prelude to the recovery of his wife, Pericles supposes for a time that he is enjoying only "the rarest dream that e'er dull sleep did mock sad fools withal." He asks the apparition,

> But are you flesh and blood?
> Have you a working pulse? And are no fairy?

Eliot's speaker asks,

> What is this face, less clear and clearer
> The pulse in the arm, less strong and stronger—
> Given or lent? more distant than stars and nearer than the eye.

The pulse may be his own, the face a vision; he next evokes

> Whispers and small laughter between leaves and hurrying feet
> Under sleep, where all the waters meet.

The sleeping and waking worlds are equivocally mingled throughout the poem, and we are not required to suppose someone passing, as Pericles did, from one to the other. A curious passage intermingling the decrepitude of his ship ("the rigging weak and the canvas rotten") with his realization that the dream-child was of his making leads into the evocation of

> This form, this face, this life
> Living to live in a world of time beyond me; let me
> Resign my life for this life, my speech for that unspoken,
> The awakened, lips parted, the hope, the new ships.

New life, new ships, and the daughter belong to the same perhaps illusory dispensation. "I made this," in the same way, points both to the ship and to the child: "between one June and another September" may or may not be a nine-month interval. The "bowsprit cracked with ice and paint cracked with heat" suggests some such lurid journey as the Ancient Mariner's, now become unsubstantial." The daughter, or the possibility of her presence, at least for the duration of Eliot's most elusive poem, suspends nerve-wracking actualities:

> What seas what shores what granite islands towards my timbers
> And woodthrush calling through the fog
> My daughter.

In *Ash-Wednesday* the woman who "moves in the time between sleep and waking" comes like the daughter in *Marina* out of the past to bestow a transitory happiness which can transfigure the world, and which after its pleasure has faded like music, leaves the world, past and present, better understood. This is the reverse of Eliot's Lazarus plot, in which someone's passing through leaves the ambience troubled. It is an event he never represents as happening at the behest of present actuality: always at the bidding of an awakened memory. Present actuality is the actuality of *Triumphal March*, or if it is subtler than that it is Bradley's "immediate experience," a circle closed on the outside.

> This is the use of memory:
> For liberation—not less of love but expanding
> Of love beyond desire, and so liberation
> From the future as well as the past . . .
> . . . See, now they vanish,
> The faces and places, with the self which, as it could, loved them,
> To become renewed, transfigured, in another pattern.
>
> *(Little Gidding)*

What we are entitled to prize in the natural present is "tension." A new verse may perhaps restore the ancient rhyme, and a verse is not only something added to a poem but etymologically a turning again; nevertheless the last section of *Ash-Wednesday* begins "Although I do not hope to turn again. . . ." The emphasis of the final prayer,

> Suffer us not to mock ourselves with falsehood
> Teach us to care and not to care
> Teach us to sit still,

is explicated by Eliot in specific terms five years later, in the play about the Canterbury Bishop who was tempted not to resist his enemies, and finally succeeded in not resisting them, but not as he had been tempted. There are ways of not caring and of sitting still that constitute mocking ourselves with falsehood. The function of the journey detailed in *Ash-Wednesday* is to arrive at a knowledge of the modes and possibilities of temporal redemption sufficient to prevent our being deluded by a counterfeit of the negative way. The 1920's were full of elegant sceptics, and T.S. Eliot was one of their heroes, but he does not return the compliment.

NORTHROP FRYE

Antique Drum

An American moving to Europe to live is likely to become more sharply aware of the "Western" context and origin of his cultural tradition, and hence to be attracted to some theory about the shape and development of that tradition. Such theories fall into two main groups, the going-up and the going-down. The going-up one started as the humanistic view, predominant from the sixteenth to the eighteenth century and implied in the title of Gibbon's *Decline and Fall*. This is a U-shaped parabola reaching its bottom with the "triumph of barbarism and religion" in the Dark Ages, and moving upward with the revival of learning. Not only Gibbon but the deeply conservative Johnson assumed a steady improvement of life and manners up to his time, an assumption which Eliot regards as a major source of Johnson's strength and security as a critic. The complementary or Romantic view is an inverted U rising to its height in medieval "Gothic" and falling off with the Renaissance, and is most articulate in Ruskin.

In the late nineteenth century the going-up parabola lost its opening curve and developed into a theory of progress, which Darwin's theory of evolution was supposed to confirm scientifically. The key to progress was the growing respect for individual freedom, making for democracy in politics, and liberalism, with a strong affinity to Protestantism, in thought. The descendant of the Ruskinian view we may call, in an image of *The Waste Land*, the bobsled or "down we went" theory. According to this, the height of civilisation was reached in the Middle Ages, when society, religion and the arts expressed a common set of standards and values. This does not mean that living conditions were better then—a point which could hardly matter less—but that the cultural synthesis of the Middle Ages symbolises an ideal of

European community. All history since represents a degeneration of this ideal. Christendom breaks down into nations, the Church into heresies and sects, knowledge into specialisations, and the end of the process is what the writer is sorrowfully contemplating in his own time: "the disintegration of Christendom, the decay of a common belief and a common culture."

This view, though held as far on the left as William Morris, is more congenial to such Catholic apologists as Chesterton, and to such literary critics as Ezra Pound, whose conception of "usura" sums up a good deal of its demonology. Eliot's social criticism, and much of his literary criticism, falls within this framework. He is uniformly opposed to theories of progress that invoke the authority of evolution, and contemptuous of writers who attempt to popularise a progressive view, like H.G. Wells. The "disintegration" of Europe began soon after Dante's time; a "diminution" of all aspects of culture has afflicted England since Queen Anne; the nineteenth century was an age of progressive "degradation"; in the last fifty years evidences of "decline" are visible in every department of human activity. Eliot adopts, too, the rhetorical device, found in Newman and others, of asserting that "There are two and only two finally tenable hypotheses about life: the Catholic and the materialistic." Everything which is neither, including Protestantism, "Whiggery," liberalism and humanism, is in between, and consequently forms a series of queasy transitional hesitations, each worse than the one before it.

We are reminded of Spengler's *Decline of the West*, a best-seller in Germany when Eliot was writing *The Waste Land*, which sees history as a series of cultures that behave like organisms, so that their decline is an inevitable ageing process. Eliot could doubtless take only the lowest view of Spengler's book, but Spengler's is the most coherent statement of the theory of Western decline, and any writer who adopts a version of that theory gets involved in Spenglerian metaphors. Thus Eliot falls into such phrases as "an age of immaturity or an age of senility," utters prophecies about "the dark ages before us" and "the barbarian nomads of the future," and incorporates references to blood and soil in his otherwise very un-Teutonic vocabulary.

Eliot belonged to one of the great dynastic New England families who have supplied so much cultural and political leadership in American life, and, like other American writers with such names as Adams and Lowell, reflects the preoccupations of an unacknowledged aristocracy, preoccupations with tradition, with breeding, with the loss of common social assumptions. "The mind resorts to reason for want of training," said Henry Adams, and Adams felt that man could worship only "silent and infinite force," either in the spiritual form of the Virgin of Chartres or in the material form of the dynamo—a close parallel to Eliot's dialectic. Eliot feels that man's natural society is not classless, but one in which "an aristocracy should have a peculiar and essential function." A functional aristocracy implies a functional peasantry. The small regional community, homogeneous in race and preferably in language, is the proper cultural unit. We are even told that "it would appear to be for the best that the great majority of human beings should go on living in the place in which they were born." In the essays on culture and Christian society much attention is paid to Welsh and Scottish cultural nationalism as a "safeguard" against the tendency "to lose their racial character." In *After Strange Gods* Eliot, addressing a Virginian audience, expresses sympathy with the conservative, neo-agrarian movement of Southern intellectuals, and remarks: "I think that the chances for the reestablishment of a native culture are perhaps better here than in New England. You are farther away from New York; you have been less industrialised and less invaded by foreign races; and you have a more opulent soil."

In the poetry the mingling of races and the sense of lost pedigree symbolise a disintegration of culture, like the ethical miscellany in "Gerontion" and the woman in *The Waste Land* who claims to be "echt deutsch" because she comes from Lithuania. A more squalid mongrelism may be represented by Sam Wauchope in *Sweeney Agonistes*, whom his American friends boast to be "a real live Britisher," but who appears to be nothing more than a Canadian. In "Gerontion" and elsewhere the Jew embodies the rootlessness of the modern metropolis, and Virginia, with a different problem on its hands, is informed that "reasons of race and religion combine to make any large number of free-thinking Jews undesirable." Behind this is a belief that "blood kinship" and attachment to the soil are features of a "harmony with nature" which a genuine society has, "unintelligible to the industrialized mind."

These features of Eliot's thought are well known, widely criticised, and for most readers fantastic or repellent. It is therefore important to realise that the historical myth behind them is not essential to his real argument. The real decline is from an ideal which may be symbolised by medieval culture, but remains in the present to condemn and challenge the contemporary world. Thus the historical myth is projected from a conception of two levels of human life which are always simultaneously present.

All views of life that Eliot would call serious or mature distinguish between two selves in man: the selfish and the self-respecting. These are not only distinguishable but opposed, and in Christianity the opposition is total, as for it the selfish self is to be annihilated, and the other is the immortal soul one is trying to save. Theories of conduct exalting the freedom of the personality or character without making this distinction are disastrous. They lead to a breakdown of community, for the ordinary or selfish self is locked in its private jail-cell, "each in his prison," its only relation to society being an

aggressive or acquisitive one. The argument of *After Strange Gods* leads up to
and concludes with an attack on the undiscriminating theory of personality.
What is admired in modern culture "tends naturally to be the *unregenerate*
personality." We thus have a lower level of ordinary or mere personality, or
what we shall loosely call the ego, and the higher level of the genuine self.
The ordinary personality is Rousseau's noble savage: it regards the community
as a limitation of its freedom, and judges the community according to the
amount of inconvenience to the ego that it causes. Eliot starts from Burke's
view that society is prior to the individual. As Burke says, art is man's nature:
the human world is a civilised one, an order of nature distinct from the
physical world. Laws for the will, beliefs for the reason, and great classics of
culture for the imagination, are there from the beginning. If a man is a
twentieth-century Englishman, he cannot claim that he is a timeless and
spaceless "I": his context cannot be separated from his real personality, which
it completes and fulfils.

　　The particular continuum into which an individual is born, Eliot calls
his culture or tradition. By culture Eliot means "that which makes life worth
living": one's total way of life, including art and education, but also cooking
and sports. By tradition, also, Eliot means both a conscious and an unconscious life in a social continuum. "What I mean by tradition involves all those
habitual actions, habits and customs . . . which represent the blood kinship of
'the same people living in the same place.'" The significance of the phrase
"blood kinship" we have already commented on. Political life may become
world-wide and depersonalised, but culture, in poetry and painting as in fine
wines, demands locality, a realised environment. Eliot stresses the feeling for
soil and local community in his essays on Virgil and Kipling, two poets who
have little in common except a popular reputation for being imperialists.

　　In Matthew Arnold's conception of culture, religion is a cultural
product, a part of which culture is the whole; hence the human value of a
religion lies mainly in the quality of its worldliness. In Eliot religion forms a
third level above human society. Its presence there guarantees Burke's distinction between a higher order of human and a lower order of physical
nature. "If this 'supernatural' is suppressed . . . the *dualism* of man and nature
collapses at once. Man is man because he can recognize supernatural realities,
not because he can invent them." Hence human culture is aligned with a
spiritual reality which is superior to it and yet within it, the kind of relationship represented in Christianity by the Incarnation. Eliot stresses the importance of this conception when he speaks of culture metaphorically as the
"incarnation" of a religion, the human manifestation of a superhuman
reality. A culture's religion "should mean for the individual and for the group
something toward which they strive, not merely something which they
possess," and it demonstrates that "the natural life and the supernatural life

have a conformity to each other which neither has with the mechanistic life."
In *After Strange Gods* Eliot uses "orthodoxy" to mean a conscious and
voluntary commitment to the religious aspect of tradition. No culture which
repudiates religion and deifies itself, like Marxist Communism, can get man
out of the squirrel-cage of the ego, though it may "on its own level" give "an
apparent meaning to life."

The genuine personality, then, is concrete man, man in the context
of certain social institutions, whether nation, church, culture or social class.
The ego or ordinary personality is an abstraction, and a parasitic by-product of
the genuine personality; it is anti-cultural and anti-traditional. But as the ego
is not the genuine self, it is really sub-human.

> The lengthened shadow of a man
> Is history, said Emerson,
> Who had not seen the silhouette
> Of Sweeney straddled in the sun.

What Emerson said was: "An institution is the lengthened shadow of a man."
In Eliot the reverse is true: the natural man or ego is the shadow of an
institution, or man in genuine society. Swift's Yahoo is pure natural man,
what man would be without institutions. Eliot's Sweeney is not a Yahoo, but
his "silhouette" reminds us of one. At the end of his essay on Baudelaire, Eliot
quotes T.E. Hulme as saying that institutions are necessary because man is
essentially bad.

An authoritarian inference from original sin is not very logical, for
those entrusted with imposing social discipline on others cannot by hypothe-
sis be any better themselves. Eliot does not say that he approves of what
Hulme says, but only that Baudelaire would have done so. But still Eliot
thinks of democracy as permeated by the natural man's admiration for
himself. What the natural man wants is only generic: food, houses, sexual
intercourse and possessions, and a society which accepts these wants as
genuine social ends becomes totalitarian. Fascism and Communism are the
products of strong tendencies within democracy itself, and our horror at these
products springs from the ego's dislike of inconvenience rather than love of
freedom. Eliot makes much of the virtue of humility, which he says in "East
Coker" provides "The only wisdom we can hope to acquire." Humility is the
opposite of pride, traditionally the essence of sin, and pride is life centered in
the ego. The "proud" attitude to social evils is to regard them as wholly
external to oneself, for oneself, in a state of pride, is not to be examined,
much less condemned. It ascribes everything it dislikes to an economic
system or political party, expects miraculous results from a transfer of power,
and is always in a revolutionary attitude.

Tradition for Eliot is far from being a cult of doing what has been done before. "Humility" is also a prerequisite of originality. The self-expression that springs from pride is more egocentric, but less individual, for the only self that can get expressed in this way is one just like everyone else. "Cousin Nancy" smokes and dances and impresses her aunts as modern, and fulfils "Waldo" Emerson's doctrine of self-reliance and "Matthew" Arnold's individualised culture, but what she does is still only fashionable conformity. The last line of this poem is quoted from Meredith's sonnet on the hopeless rebellion of Lucifer, and aligns Nancy with the same futility.

For most people acceptance of culture and tradition is unconscious, expressed in assumption and prejudice. A man is hardly a human being at all until he has entered a tradition, or what some call a social contract. But "What is important is a structure of society in which there will be, from 'top' to 'bottom,' a continuous gradation of cultural levels . . . we should not consider the upper levels as possessing *more* culture than the lower, but as representing a more conscious culture and a greater specialization of culture." There should be, therefore, an "élite" of those for whom culture and tradition have become conscious. They include poets for at least two reasons. First, "poetry differs from every other art in having a value for the people of the poet's race and language, which it can have for no other." Second, "unless we have those few men who combine an exceptional sensibility with an exceptional power over words, our own ability, not merely to express, but even to feel any but the crudest emotions, will degenerate." They also include critics, who depend on "a settled society" "in which the difference of religious and political views are not extreme." This last implies that the élite should have a close connexion with the culture's religion.

Religion sees human life in relation to superhuman life, as a kind of continuous imitation of it. This is expressed in certain acts, or sacraments, and in certain forms of thought, or dogmas derived from revelation. Religion cannot be identical with culture, except in the City of God or in a very primitive society; but if religion and culture draw apart, society loses its sense of direction, and the élite and the unreflecting masses become unintelligible to each other. Eliot's conception of religion is thus a sacramental and catholic one: the church is the definitive form of ritual and faith, and the essence of religion is participation in the church. Protestant conceptions of the church would doubtless not be admissible to Eliot if we could suppose he knew what they were. When he says "the life of Protestantism depends upon the survival of that against which it protests," we are apparently to take this lugubrious pun as representing his understanding of the faith that the head of his church defends.

Eliot's élite are interpreters of their society, and show that what is most deliberately and consciously cultured in any society is also central to it, and guides its main current. Eliot, like Arnold, feels that "the dissentients must remain marginal," even when they form the majority. For Eliot admits, even stresses, that we can have an *Athanasius contra mundum* situation in which "the man who is 'representative' of his time may be in opposition to the most widely-accepted beliefs of his time." If Athanasius is right, he is in the "centre" of his society; if he is wrong or partly right, he is "marginal." Neither Eliot nor Arnold, has explored the difficulties in this metaphor very far. Eliot's élite is similar, as he recognises, to Coleridge's "clerisy," but Eliot's argument is more pro-Catholic, stressing the importance of contemplative orders in the church. Coleridge's differences from him on these points "now sound merely quaint." In Eliot, as again in Arnold, the Establishment is society's recognition both of the centrality of the church and of the distinction between the church and the marginal sects. Of disestablishment Eliot says: "the risks are so great that such an act can be nothing but a desperate measure"—a strong statement for a poet brought up in the United States.

It follows that education should have the socially engaged personality as its goal. One type of education, distinguished by Eliot as instruction or information, is designed to provide the ego with extended powers. This type usually depends on a socially subversive theory aiming at transforming society by equality of opportunity. The fable of the belly and members is replaced in Eliot by an analogy of the head and trunk of the body politic. We feel that we are members of one body when the culture of a minority is the conscious form of the culture of the majority. Education should aim at a social ideal like Newman's gentleman, whose leisure and good taste are produced by an awareness of social context rather than by class privilege or private enterprise. Arnold's conception of culture is evaluative, the *best* that has been thought and said, and as such plays a revolutionary role in society. "Culture seeks to do away with classes," and the permeation of society by culture tends toward equality. In Eliot the conception of culture is descriptive, hence it plays no revolutionary role. The classes of the past may give place to the élites of the future, but culture itself does nothing to disturb the class structure.

Eliot's literary criticism falls into two parts, a literary polemic derived from the myth of decline and a critical theory derived from the study and practice of literature. The former is what concerns us here.

The progressive view of history produced the post-Romantic conception of English literature which Eliot challenged. According to this, originality in poetry is an aspect of individual freedom in life; hence Shakespeare, who drew individuals so well, and Milton, a Protestant revolutionary, express the real genius of English literature. The era from Dryden to Johnson was an inferior and prosier age, but the Romantic movement reestablished the main tradition, which continued in Britain through Tennyson and Swinburne, and in America through Whitman's conception of poetry as self-expression.

Eliot's historical view of English literature is a point-for-point reversal of the progressive one. The post-Romantic conception of "personality," failing to distinguish the craftsman from the ordinary personality, assumes that the former is the medium or vehicle of the latter, instead of the other way round. In "Tradition and the Individual Talent" Eliot speaks of the poetic process as "impersonal," not an expression of personality but an "escape" from it. The poet's mind is a place where something happens to words, like a catalyser which accompanies but does not manipulate a chemical action. In other early essays, though Eliot agrees with Arnold about the immaturity of the Romantic poets, he means by "Romanticism" chiefly the popular post-Romantic residue of their influence which is contemporary with himself. This Romanticism, he says, "leads its disciples only back upon themselves." Romanticism, then, as a creative process emanating from and returning to the ego, occupies the foreground of Eliot's historical dialectic, the contemporary world at the bottom of the Western mountain, as far as we can get from the "anti-romantic" "practical sense of realities" in Dante's *Vita Nuova*.

The First World War discredited the view that the northern, liberal, largely Protestant cultures of England and Germany were, with America, the architects of a new world. Latin and Catholic Europe began to look like a cultural as well as a political ally. The essay on Blake in *The Sacred Wood* is full of anti-Nordic mythology: Blake's prophecies "illustrate the crankiness, the eccentricity, which frequently affects writers outside of the Latin tradition." So although Eliot's view of literature is "classical," his Classicism regards Latin medieval culture, and Dante in particular, as the culmination of the Classical achievement. Dante's greatness is partly a product of a time when Europe "was mentally more united than we can now conceive." At such a time literature achieves its greatest power and clarity: "there is an opacity, or inspissation of poetic style throughout Europe after the Renaissance." So Eliot explicitly prefers the culture which produced Dante to that which produced Shakespeare.

Eliot reiterates that Shakespeare is as great a poet as Dante, but, reflecting an age nearer ours, the materials out of which his poetry is made are shoddier. "Dante made great poetry out of a great philosophy of life; and Shakespeare made equally great poetry out of an inferior and muddled philosophy of life." Eliot, like Shaw, finds Shakespeare's philosophy of life a mass of platitudes with a pessimistic slant, and agrees with Archer that Elizabethan drama is an "impure art," though his moral is the opposite of Archer's belief in "progress . . . and in the superiority and efficiency of the present age." He also agrees with Arnold that Shakespeare is too clever to have a good effect on tradition. "If you try to imitate Shakespeare you will certainly produce a series of stilted, forced, and violent distortions of language." The conclusion is that we should admire Shakespeare, but not for liberal or Romantic reasons. Shakespeare does not always take a maturely dim view of human nature: his rhetoric may yield to his hero's desire to "see himself in a dramatic light," as Othello does in his Aleppo speech, where he shows a lack of humility. We are told that *Hamlet*, the Bible of the Romantics, is "most certainly an artistic failure," and (in two grinning footnotes) that Rymer, the seventeenth-century critic who called *Othello* a bloody farce, "makes out a very good case."

The reader may be confused by the suggestion that Shakespeare made his poetry "out of" a philosophy, whether profound or what Eliot calls "ragbag." Eliot establishes three main philosophical connexions with Shakespeare, the Cerberus of the modern world raising its heads. The ancestor of modern sceptical liberalism is Montaigne, to whom Shakespeare owed much (here Eliot may have been over-influenced by J.M. Robertson, as he was in his *Hamlet* essay by Robertson's disintegrating fantasies). The ancestor of Romantic egoism is Seneca the Stoic, whose conception of the hero seems like a cult of spiritual pride. The ancestry of the secularism that ends in expediency is in the cynical political views ascribed by the Elizabethans to Machiavelli. Machiavelli himself said that unscrupulousness in politics is necessary because men are "ungrateful, fickle, false, cowards, covetous," which sounds like a belief in original sin, hence "In Machiavelli there is no cynicism whatever."

Eliot's political attitude is said in the preface to *For Lancelot Andrewes* to be "royalist." Royalism for Eliot, as for Burke, could well mean the maintaining of a symbol of continuity in society clear of party politics or class struggle. But though Eliot announced an *Outline of Royalism* and speaks of the divine right of kings as a "noble faith," the conception has little importance in his work except as an indication that he was taking a side in the seventeenth-century civil war. Much of Eliot's criticism revolves around the first part of the seventeenth century, a period he approaches as one which contains in embryo all the disintegrating tendencies of our time. Shakespeare, Tourneur and Jonson can still control them while reflecting them, but Massinger and Ford are beginning to yield to them. Then came the Civil War, the Puritan emigrations, including the Eliots from East Coker, the closing of the theatres, the overthrow of everything catholic in the Church of England from the Little Gidding community to Archbishop Laud, and the poetry of Milton. With all this the tradition of English culture fell to pieces, and the modern world was born. For anyone concerned to oppose the tendencies of that world, "the Civil War is not ended," as Eliot was still insisting as late as 1947.

Milton was a poet of the devil's party and at least the devil probably knew it. He subjected the language to a deterioration which meant that on later writing his influence could only be for the worse. He built a "Chinese wall" across poetry, the work of a man imaginatively as well as physically blind, showing a vague visual sense and leading nowhere "outside of the mazes of sound." His rhetoric is that of "the greatest of all eccentrics," valid only for Milton himself, an apotheosis of the ego. It is full of tricks like "the facile use of resonant names" which Marlowe outgrew, and Marlowe's Mephistopheles "renders Milton's Satan superfluous." Johnson was right in finding *Lycidas* full of "absurdities"; *L'Allegro* and *Il Penseroso* are on a level with "the lighter and less successful poems of Keats"; Swinburne is praised for abusing *Comus*, which is also called "the death of the masque."

With Dryden the real tradition was to some degree reestablished, for it is "easier to get back to healthy language from Dryden." Though Eliot admires Pope and does what he can to rehabilitate Dryden and Johnson as poets and critics, he does not maintain that the Augustan age produced a poet of the stature of, say, Racine in France. Of the Romantics, those who best illustrate the egocentric quality of Romanticism are Byron and Shelley. The fact that Shelley, as a man, was "self-centred, and sometimes almost a blackguard" is relevant, because although "Wordsworth does not present a very pleasing personality either," Shelley's "abuse of poetry" is greater. Byron's egoism is connected with the "defective sensibility" which made him write English like a dead language. Blake's work is egocentric because it contains a philosophy which Blake thought out himself instead of borrowing from his tradition. In reputation the biggest figure in this period is Goethe, and Goethe "dabbled in both philosophy and poetry and made no great success of either."

Contemporary literature is of course full of the detritus of Romanticism. "Religion and Literature," an essay unlikely ever to rank with *Areopagitica* as a ringing manifesto of intellectual freedom, says that "while individual modern writers of eminence can be improving, contemporary literature as a whole tends to be degrading." Hardy is "a powerful personality uncurbed by any institutional attachment," who expressed that personality without having anything "particularly wholesome or edifying" to express. D.H. Lawrence's "vision is spiritual, but spiritually sick." Yeats, with his little-Ireland folklore and his occultism, has a minor and peripheral mythology. (So did the Hebrew prophets and Christian apostles, but, as explained above, they were really central, because right.) Elsewhere we find slighting references to Bernard Shaw, H.G. Wells, and Bertrand Russell. These are prose writers, and "good prose cannot be written by a people without convictions." What convictions they are also seems to be important. Our attention is called "to the great excellence of Bishop Hensley Henson's prose," but we are told that Russell, in his quasi-Stoical *A Free Man's Worship*, wrote "bad prose."

"We all agree about the 'cultural breakdown'," says Eliot, but myths of decline usually have a codicil: the writer has something contemporary to recommend which promises to arrest the decline of civilization. Eliot himself points out that his historical dialectic, on its literary side, is attached to a tactical campaign to get new types of writing recognised. Of the writers he defends, Ezra Pound and James Joyce are the most prominent. Romantic, Protestant and liberal tendencies in the English tradition make it more culturally schismatic than the French tradition, where Racine and Baudelaire "are in some ways more like each other than they are like anyone else," and which is closer to the Latin centre of European culture. It is significant that Pound and Joyce reflect the influence of Latin and Catholic civilisation, and significant too that their cultural conservatism seems to go with originality of expression. The discovery, with the belated publication of the poetry of Hopkins, that the most disturbingly original Victorian poet was a Jesuit priest looked like confirmation of the same priniciple, but in *After Strange Gods* Eliot refuses to play this ace and finesses with Joyce, the "most ethically orthodox writer" of our time.

Eliot's skill in quotation and in setting passages of unequal merit beside each other put his handling of his critical polemic on an unusually high level of objectivity. Only occasionally can we see the rhetorical shading of the arguments. In the final canto of the *Inferno* we come upon Dante's Satan, with three heads, one of which is meditatively chewing Judas Iscariot. The uninstructed reader might find the scene a trifle barbaric, and feel that what Milton did with Satan was more civilised. Eliot, recognising the danger, says: "The vision of Satan may seem grotesque, especially if we have fixed in our minds the curly-haired Byronic hero of Milton." This remark is too remote from Milton to be even misleading: it is sheer polemic and nothing more. In his essay on Sir John Davies, Eliot sets a passage from *Orchestra* beside one from *The Ancient Mariner* containing the line "His great bright eye most silently," and says parenthetically that "most" is a blemish. Considering that *The Ancient Mariner* is a deliberate imitation of ballad idiom, with its bits of metrical putty, it is perhaps not a blemish. But a sense of the superiority of pre-Romantic craftsmanship has been quietly implanted in the reader's mind.

With the Second World War and the completion of "Little Gidding," the Civil War reached an armistice on its last battlefield. Eliot, Pound and Joyce were by that time established writers. In later essays the polemical tone is abandoned, the Romantics are referred to without much animus, and the terms classic and romantic are now said to belong to "literary politics." A second essay on Milton holds a cautious Geiger counter up to that poet and decides that "at last" it is safe for poets to read him. In pointing out that Milton can hardly have been a worse influence on later epic than Shakespeare on later verse drama, Eliot comes close to saying that every major poet builds a "Chinese wall"—a principle that will in due course be applied to Eliot himself. "That every great work of poetry tends to make impossible the production of equally great works of the same kind is indisputable." The greater urbanity sometimes goes with a loss of incisiveness. "I should myself rate Campion as a more important poet than Herrick, though very much below Herbert" sounds amateurish compared to an earlier statement that the critic's task is to isolate quality, not to determine rank.

The best comment on Eliot's polemic is that of his mentor in "Little Gidding": "These things have served their purpose; let them be." We may consider applying to Eliot his own early comment that Arnold "went for game outside of the literary preserve altogether," which "we must regret," because it "might perhaps have been carried on as effectively, if not quite so neatly, by some disciple (had there been one) in an editorial position on a newspaper." Certainly when we read in *The Idea of a Christian Society*: "It is a matter of concern not only in this country, but has been mentioned with concern by the late Supreme Pontiff . . . that the masses of the people have become increasingly alienated from Christianity," we may wonder if it really needed a writer of Eliot's abilities to produce that sentence. A poet's specific task has something to do with visualising the Promised Land: on the historical level, he may often be a lost leader, a Moses floundering in a legal desert. As Eliot says, it is the Word in the desert that is most likely to hear "The loud lament of the disconsolate chimera." It is difficult to feel that Eliot's view of Western culture is anything more than a heresy in his own sense of the word, a partial insight with "a seductive simplicity" which is "altogether more plausible than the truth." The orthodoxy of which it is a heresy would be, or include, a much larger "truth" about our very complex situation than the mythology of decline affords. Nevertheless, the construct from which Eliot's social criticism is projected is also that of his poetry, hence it illuminates our understanding of his poetry and its relation to his own time.

JAMES OLNEY

Four Quartets:
"Folded in a Single Party"

Any reader of Eliot will recognize
that to call the *Four Quartets* autobiographic poetry requires some considerable explanation and qualification. It would unquestionably be an easier
thing to establish the autobiographic elements of, for example, the *Prelude* or
Yeats' Tower poem than of *Four Quartets*. But in the very ease with which we
can identify Wordsworth's conscious life with his poem there is the temptation to rest content with natural geography and chronology, with poetic
pictures neatly illustrating an educational text in moral development, and to
suppose that these represent the subject of the poem; to suppose that what
Wordsworth knows about himself and can tell us, with clear psychological
comprehension and at great explanatory length, will serve well enough for
the "bios" in autobiography. Or if one were to take Yeats's poems, which
probably represent a richer material in self-expression than either the *Prelude*
or the *Quartets*, there is the danger of being distracted by the poet's flair, by
what he said and did in the world of men, by his "circus animals" and his troop
of friends put on display regularly as partial symbols for the whole poet
himself; there is the danger of listening too much to Yeats's own description of
himself and his soul, delivered brilliantly both in and out of the poems, and of
listening with such delighted fascination that we are distracted from the
poetic self that is only in the poem and that is the only self relevant in
discussing autobiographic art.

> There was a Boy: ye knew him well, ye cliffs
> And islands of Winander!—many a time
> At evening. . . .
>
> (*Prelude*, V, 364-66)

From *Metaphors of Self: The Meaning of Autobiography*. Copyright © 1972 by Princeton
University Press.

One never gets this sort of Wordsworthian natural geography and exterior biography in Eliot; nor does Eliot refer freely to his offices in Russell Square as Yeats does lavishly to his Tower near Gort and to its winding stair, its broken battlements, and the stream flowing by. What sparse personal reference there is and what little geography (the four place names, for example), or what few events figure in the *Quartets*, are plainly, on first occurrence, supernatural or extra-mundane and do not require to be transformed from the natural realm either by the poet's explanation or the reader's symbolizing imagination. It may be, however, that this lack, this absence of the persons, the possessions, the places, and the happenings of a particular life, motivated apparently both by personal reticence and poetic strategy, will prove in the end, for our purposes, a virtue rather than a defect; that if we must go very carefully in seeking Eliot's subject, the care will provide its own critical reward. I have never seen, but can well imagine, an illustrated *Prelude*, and photographs of Yeats country and of his symbols are easy enough to come by; but I cannot quite conceive of any photographic images that might usefully accompany the *Quartets*. The chapel at Little Gidding is no doubt interesting, but a picture of it would help very little in reading that poem. I am not sure that this is all to the bad. In any case, when one says that the *Quartets* are "auto-biographic," that does not at all mean that in them will be found datable, placeable, perhaps photographable, events.

Four *Quartets* is not, however we look at it, an imitation of events but, if an imitation at all, then of something quite different: perhaps an imitation of a process. Poetry that is expressive and autobiographic in a deeper than personalistic or historic sense draws metaphors, or accepts and adopts them, from the self as it is becoming, and then displays all the world to the reader through the glass of these metaphors. It does not submit to the fixed and, as we call them, objective forms of a pre-existent universe, but, insofar as it treats these external lineaments, transforms them into expressive vehicles of subjective emotions and private consciousness. In a general way, this is the mode of the *Quartets*, and their one great subject, lying well below the surface of the poem and hardly remarked in most critical writing on it, subsuming and informing all secondary interests (e.g., poetry, history, philosophy, religion), is the evolving self: that self which is the determining subject, or subjective center, of all creativity, and is the great subject-object of the creations of Jung and Montaigne as well as of Eliot.

Four *Quartets* has been called "philosophic poetry," and I think that, with necessary definitions, one might accept this as a working description. This is not at all, however, the same thing as saying that, as one commentator puts it, "Eliot has sought to vindicate the ways of God to man. The *Quartets*, a new *Essay on Man*, are the poetic jottings of a philosophy holding that the world is an organ of the divine purpose." Eliot may very well have believed this about the world; who can say? But I am sure that his poem has no resemblance at all to the *Essay on Man*, nor is it "poetic jottings" of any kind, nor does it contain anything like a philosophy. "Philosophic" is merely an adjective, suggesting some of the characteristic interests of the poem: but the proper substantive is "poetry." To assume that the poem aspires to the discipline of philosophy but fails and so collapses into "poetic jottings" is to take hold of the wrong end of the stick and beat the poem with it. Moreover, if we thus consider the poem to be philosophy *manqué*, we not only do the poem an injustice but ourselves as well, for in so doing we shut ourselves out, as readers, from what is there in fact and of great value. I.A. Richards, speaking both as a friend of the poet and as a critic of the poetry, comes much closer to the true essence of the *Quartets*: "Few minds," he says of Eliot, "have more enjoyed the process of pondering a discrimination: pondering it rather than formulating it or maintaining it." The discriminations that Eliot ponders in the *Four Quartets* are mostly to be described as "philosophic," but the poetry is in the intensity with which Eliot realizes the pondering not in the neatness or finality with which he arranges his philosophy. One might say that pondering is not only the mode but, in a sense, the subject as well of the poem. In any case, the pondering proves to be a circular process that does not issue in an answer but turns in upon itself for substance, and Eliot never, speaking in his own voice, formulates a philosophy or maintains a conclusion. Indeed, I am not sure that we can say that Eliot ever speaks in his own voice in *Four Quartets*, and if he does not, then that fact is of great importance.

If we consider such a passage as this, which has the same feeling about it as a good many passages in the poem,

> Whisper of running streams, and winter lightning.
> The wild thyme unseen and the wild strawberry,
> The laughter in the garden, echoed ecstasy. . . .
> (EC, III, 29-31)

there can be no question that *Four Quartets* is, in an important way, an expression of personal emotion; that it is, in other words, lyric poetry. But to whom, one must ask, is the emotion "personal"? Who is the "person" of the poem? Again, it is reasonable to say that it is, in part, "meditative verse" as Eliot describes that: "the voice of the poet talking to himself—or to nobody" (*On Poetry and Poets*, p. 106). But is it exactly or only the poet who is talking in the *Four Quartets*? I would suggest that the poem presents us with something different and something more; that it is a dramatized meditation pursued by one who is both Eliot and other than Eliot, and that in being so it avails itself of many of the virtues of dramatic poetry without surrendering those of meditative verse.

Let me give an example: in the second section of "Little Gidding" the speaker of the poem and "a familiar compound ghost / Both intimate and unidentifiable" meet and tread "the pavement in a dead patrol," talking philosophically of things past, passing, and to come. The identity of this ghost has naturally vexed Eliot criticism a great deal: it is said to be Yeats and Joyce, both dead a few years since, their bodies "left . . . on a distant shore"— or even Shelley, by the same evidence; but the ghost has also been identified as partly Pound, not at all dead of course, and partly Swift, with a considerable admixture of Milton and Dante and an important phrase from Mallarmé. Undoubtedly there are others dancing together in this complete consort of a ghost as well. But might one not also, and perhaps more fruitfully, consider it to be past Eliots; for is that not what a compound ghost would be—a congeries of spirits standing for our heritage and our ancestral significant moments; a collection of disembodied souls representing our personal, professional, national, human past and informing our individual present? "So I assumed a double part," the voice of the poem says,

> . . . and cried
> And heard another's voice cry: "What! are *you* here?"
> Although we were not. I was still the same,
> Knowing myself yet being someone other. . . .

Is this Eliot speaking? Well, yes, in a sense; but not Eliot alone, or not only the Eliot of the present historic moment. It is what Eliot has been in the past and what he is becoming into the future, speaking in "another's voice" and surprised to hear his own speech. Likewise, the ghost is known and unknown, figures from the past and a figure becoming for the future, himself and another:

> And he a face still forming; yet the words sufficed
> To compel the recognition they preceded.
> And so, compliant to the common wind,
> Too strange to each other for misunderstanding,
> In concord at this intersection time
> Of meeting nowhere, no before and after,
> We trod the pavement in a dead patrol.

The speaker in this section, and this is more or less true throughout the *Quartets*, is Eliot and not Eliot, the ghost is Eliot and more than Eliot, the street is in London, in history, and in purgatory, and the action is a fully dramatized meditation in a supernatural, transfigured setting of an "intersection time" when chronological relation is replaced by significant relation and geographic location by nonspatial intensity.

In search of the "person" or the "voice" of *Four Quartets*, it seems to me that Eliot, insofar as he is the speaker of the poem, could be said to be almost an anonymous lyric poet and the poem an expression of depersonalized or transpersonalized personal emotion. It seems, indeed, natural, in discussion of the *Quartets*, to refer to "the poet" rather than to "Eliot," which is evidence of his success in making the emotional experience of the poem anonymous. A suggestive analogy might be made with certain Middle English lyrics (e.g., "Alison" or "Lenten ys come with love to toune") where the voice, by historical chance but also in tone and treatment, is in fact anonymous, and the emotion of seasonal revitalization rendered in the poem becomes, by that fact, both specifically individual and anonymously, comprehensively human. Likewise, the speaker of *Four Quartets*: without ever ceasing to be individual—indeed, becoming individual by the process of the poem—he enacts a representative drama, very much like Montaigne's drama, of spiritual man in meditation. Through this "anonymification," *Four Quartets* succeeds in being both more and less personal than earlier poems such as "Prufrock" or "Gerontion" in which Eliot created "type" figures— i.e., individually coherent personae not to be totally identified with, but also not to be totally separated from, the poet speaking through them. In the *Quartets*, however, the poet has submerged his self sufficiently in the general experience of mankind that he may return to the personal "I" and "we" and find therein not the historic and typical but the representative and symbolic.

If one calls *Four Quartets* "philosophic poetry," then one should be very careful at the same time to recognize that the poem is not at all an ordered (or worse, disordered), single-minded presentation of *a* philosophy; and as long as we see it as a dramatic poem of the self we shall, as we must, avoid confusing it with a poeticized philosophy like the *Essay on Man*. The "truths" that are pondered in the enacted communication of section II of "Little Gidding" are not absolute and objective but relative and subjective: truths that take their coherence and effectiveness from the intensity of the artist's imagination and realization of them rather than from their own inherent validity as a discursive explanation of the external universe. "A philosophical theory," Eliot wrote in 1921, "which has entered into poetry is established, for its truth or falsity in one sense ceases to matter, and its truth in another sense is proved." What he means, of course, is that the theory is established as drama and as poetry without regard for its truth or falsity as philosophy; the poem is validated in the reader's imagination not in the external world. *Four Quartets* goes even further than this as dramatic poetry, subjectively centered in the artist's and the reader's imagination: the embodied conflict of the *Quartets'* drama engages thoughts and emotions rather than ideas and characters; it enacts a pondering rather than a theory. Thoughts, unlike ideas and theory, cannot be separated from the mind that thinks them, and the poem concerns itself with the working of the mind, not with its separable, formulated products; with the process of the psyche, not with ideas or theory as such. Putting the matter in Jung's language, one might say that *Four Quartets* is the autobiography not of ego-consciousness alone, though of course the portrait includes that, nor of the external person and his acts, but of the whole psyche and self. The feelings of the *Four Quartets* are too complex for simply rational language, and the thoughts of the poem do often lie too deep, if not for tears, at least for intellectual articulation.

"I am certain," Keats says, speaking as an artist, "of nothing but of the holiness of the Heart's affections and the truth of Imagination—What the imagination seizes as Beauty must be truth—whether it existed before or not." Eliot claimed, with what I take to be a sort of prim, intellectual humility, not to understand the end of the "Ode on a Grecian Urn," and one cannot be sure that he would have been any warmer in his enthusiasm for what Keats says here; but it is the "truth of Imagination" that *Four Quartets* establishes, and the poem depends upon the creative powers of the imagination for realizing its own proper object. That object—"Beauty," as Keats calls it—will *be* as intensely as the poet and reader can make it be, "whether it existed before or not." Speaking of religious belief, but also as an artist rather than a priest, Tolstoy says much the same thing as Keats: "As my body has descended to me from God, so also has my reason and my understanding of life, and consequently the various stages of the development of that understanding of life cannot be false. All that people sincerely believe in must be true; it may be differently expressed but it cannot be a lie, and therefore if it presents itself to me as a lie, that only means that I have not understood it." All that people sincerely believe in must be true": it is characteristic of Tolstoy that his expression should be a bit strong for many tastes and that some readers who might otherwise be friendly enough to his brand of solipsism would shy away from the extremity of this remark. But let us consider whether, given his premises, which may not prove so outrageous or unusual, Tolstoy might not be more perceptive and exact in his statement than we would ordinarily want to admit; and whether Tolstoy's premises are not, in fact, rather close to Eliot's as the author of the *Quartets*. If, as Tolstoy said in a hundred different ways, we are all of us instances of Godhead incarnate; if, in our consciousness, and only there so far as the created universe is concerned, the divine realizes itself; if what we "sincerely believe" is our deepest imagination and our best apprehension of that realized divinity that we experience as a personal, subjective state—then it is not hyperbole but in fact the merest tautology to say that "All that people sincerely believe in must be true." How could it *not* be true? It is God believing in himself and causing himself to be as sincerely and as intensely as he can, given the imaginative, believing limitations of the individual through whom the belief is effected. I do not suppose that the Eliot who was "classicist in literature, royalist in politics, and anglo-Catholic in religion," and who exercised himself so vehemently against the "Inner Light" ("the most untrustworthy and deceitful guide that ever offered itself to wandering humanity") and against the *"personal view of life"* that, he claimed, constituted the heresy of modern writers and modern literature, would care to go that way with Tolstoy—who, after all, was romantic-realist in literature, anarchist in politics, and excommunicated heretic in religion, and who never followed anything *but* his Inner Light. Yet, the fact I think is that the Eliot who wrote *Four Quartets* did go that way in the poem; or at least the poem goes that way for the reader whatever Eliot, the man of prose and of religious and literary orthodoxy, might have desired.

What Tolstoy says about belief makes of religion, as of philosophy and psychology, a creative act in self-knowledge. For the artist, I should think, this is more apparently and more indisputably the case than for the theologian. Absolute standards of truth or falsity against which to measure the artist's creation do not exist, for it is his creation, made out of his subjective experience. When the poem not only begins, like all poetry, in the poet's "own emotions" but, as I believe to be the case with the *Four Quartets*, turns inside out and embraces that private experience in awareness as its very subject or object, then even relative standards of truth and falsity are somewhat beside the point in reading and judging the poem. Here again, in this turn and return on the self, the difference between the *Essay on Man* and the *Four Quartets* is crucial. As readers without a yardstick and a poem that anyhow refuses to stay to be measured, we can only look within: we must judge the poem by how adequately it answers, not to the external universe, not even to the poet's experience—since we have no knowledge of that—but to our own experience; not the surface experience of everyday activities either, but the deepest experience of what it means to us to be human beings and to be ourselves.

"Why, for all of us," Eliot asks, "out of all that we have heard, seen, felt, in a lifetime, do certain images recur, charged with emotion, rather than others?" He mentions several such mysterious and significant-feeling images, apparently from personal experience—"the leap of one fish . . . the scent of one flower, an old woman on a German mountain path," etc.—and then continues: "such memories may have symbolic value, but of what we cannot tell, for they come to represent the depths of feeling into which we cannot peer." Describing here the image-material of poetry, Eliot adopts a figurative language strikingly similar to the myths and metaphors that depth psychology employs when that "science" tries to evoke some sense of psychic process; he, like the psychiatric workers of that deep mine, speaks of reaching darkly into the depths of emotional experience where conscious mind cannot go but

whence images, rhythms, auditory excitations, all the by-products and expressions of an organic being in operation, are thrown up to affect and to be
remarked, to rhythms, it was Balzac, as realistic a novelist as the world has
ever seen, dedicated to the search for reality inherent in external appearance,
who said (in the person of his archetypal artist Frenhofer in *Le Chef-d'oeuvre
inconnu*), "La mission de l'art n'est pas de copier la nature mais de l'exprimer."
The nature that Balzac's own art expressed in the hundreds of characters he
created was, of course, that human nature that he knew, in all its diversity,
literally from within: the *Comédie humaine*, like Shakespeare's plays, represents a massive self-expression through the varied forms of human nature. In a
rhythmic variation on a passage quoted earlier—

> The distraction fit, lost in a shaft of sunlight,
> The wild thyme unseen, or the winter lightning
> Or the waterfall, or music heard so deeply
> That it is not heard at all, but you are the music
> While the music lasts.—
>
> (DS, V, 25-29)

Eliot finds in the sensory forms of nature sufficient expression for subjective
states, in particular for those moments of completion and of ecstasy when the
self is reborn anew. In the subtle, pervasive smell of thyme and the implied
taste of the herb, in the warm feel of sunlight and the chilly sight of winter
lightning, in the sound of the waterfall, in all of these, alone and together,
the self finds its metaphors. While they are all there, of course, in nature and
now in the poem, they mean nothing until we bring their meaning to them,
until in our awareness they complete and represent our whole being and so lift
that being out of itself into another pattern and onto another level of
existence and significance. In music and poetry there is something added that
the natural forms do not, in themselves and alone, necessarily possess—
rhythmic organization: the pattern that the poet finds in himself and projects
over nature and then, finding it in nature, uses to express the self that has
thereby come into being. So too the reader: after we read and become, in our
moment, the poem, then we imagine the natural forms always to have had
the pattern and the rhythms we now discover; but that is only because we see
nature through the metaphoric glass and by the senses of the self artistically
transformed. We are the poem as we read it, as the words, the images, and the
rhythms pervade and become our being; the poem stands for us, and not for us
a moment since or a moment hence but now as the images lie in the mind's
eye and penetrate the mind's ear, as the subtle rhythms go below the
conscious mind to recreate for us the same new-born self that they express. As
that self is the poet's and not the poet's, so it is ours and not ours; perhaps it is
most properly to be called the self of the poem—requiring both poet and

reader, as they require it, to come into unified being. Thus it is that in "analyzing" *Four Quartets*, one is not taking apart an external thing; "analysis" here is much more like fingering the springs of one's own being—that being that only exists as it becomes with the process of the poem.

The *Quartets* have in common with the *Essays* of Montaigne this great capacity: to be new and different in every moment that the reader responds to them. For the voice of the *Quartets*, for the "I" of the *Essays*, and for the reader, the consciousness that lies behind and around the creation, that seeks and finds words and sounds and metaphors for experience, is a constantly renewed thing, a quality continually "aborning," a state different at every point, and especially at the end (if there is an end), from what it was the moment before. It is no exaggeration to say—indeed, I think Eliot's poem every minute proves—that these expressive discoveries are as new and surprising for the poet as for his reader; and, which is to say the same thing, that they are entirely new and surprising each time one really returns to the poem, with all one is and not just with the eye. Not that our consciousness takes on philosophic substance but that it formally expands in its questioning and meditating and discovering. It is precisely this expanding, evolving consciousness that the poem both contains and expresses, both is and means. The poet, finding metaphors that increase awareness as they express it, formalizes the reader's experience equally with his own and brings coherence to both. Because this coming to consciousness has not happened but is happening in us, the poem never presents us with ordinary autobiographic description. How could it? Instead of resurrecting old counters from past experience and moving them around a new board, the poem performs, for its creator and its re-creator, the very imaginative, self-explorative process that it is about. Thus, the mode of the *Quartets* is not to discover truth and to present it, but to pursue and to create it, and not to create it outside the pursuit but within it. And in his re-creation, the reader, in effect, becomes the pursuit, the pondering, the process, the poem.

"This," in the *Quartets*, "is the use of memory": to free ourselves from the limitations of egotism by revealing the whole pattern of history in which the whole pattern of the self has been and is involved. Finding in our own actions the instincts and the necessities of humanity, we move from selfish attachment through the detachment of historic perspective, finally back to the central self that has succeeded in ordering history in its own image; that self being reintegrated now according to its newly created pattern.

> See, now they vanish,
> The faces and places, with the self which, as it could, loved them,
> To become renewed, transfigured, in another pattern.
> (LG, III, 14-16)

Thus the creative moment, whether God in his world, the poet in his poem, or the individual in his self, is the great, continuing act of love that produces something never to be lost from the sum of the universe. We may not, in our divided state, see its eternity, but any creation, divine, artistic, or individual, as Los informs us in Blake's *Milton*, is forever:

> The generations of men run on in the tide of Time,
> But leave their destin'd lineaments permanent for ever & ever.

Again like Montaigne, the speaker or philosophizer of *Four Quartets*, who is also us, embodies and proves a dramatic truth but only questions philosophic truth. As readers of the *Essays* or the *Quartets*, we have no more knowledge at the end than at the beginning; but we see things differently and we relate things in different ways not because they have at all changed but because we have, and because there exists now a new metaphor for our self. The *Four Quartets* present as little of "a philosophy" as the *Essays*. "The poet who 'thinks,'" Eliot says in an essay of 1927, "is merely the poet who can express the emotional equivalent of thought." *Four Quartets* is an intense evocation of how it feels to pursue such thought as we call philosophic, an intensely realized metaphor and dramatization of what it is like to meditate. "The term, Philosophy," according to Coleridge, who was speaking of his own activities, but he describes equally well the practice of either Montaigne or Eliot, "defines itself as an affectionate seeking after the truth; but Truth is the correlative of Being." In this way the material of *Four Quartets*, even "what the poet starts from" and what he ends with, is not Truth in an absolute, capitalized sense, but "an affectionate seeking after the truth," which is a lower-case word, a subjective fact, and a relative experience. In the process of becoming aware and of expanding consciousness, the poet, with his reader, comes into a unified state of being in the poem; and the correlative of being (perhaps not an "objective correlative" but a subjective one), as Coleridge says, is truth, which will be as intensely there in the poem— the truth of the poem, nothing else—as the self or the being brought to consciousness.

It is odd and interesting, also I think significant, that three men as distinct and different in their conscious and public personalities and in their "works and days" as T.S. Eliot, Michel de Montaigne, and C.G. Jung, should have found, beyond the reach of discursive language but not beyond the evocative powers of metaphor, style, and myth, the same essential subject: the whole self-in-becoming. Of the *Four Quartets* one might say yet more: that in them the poet combines the intuitive depth of the mystic's vision with the sensory delicacy of the scientist's observation and the structural inevitability of the logician's syllogism, the complete consort dancing together to the rhythm of the emotions and of the unconscious, to realize the complete pattern of self. And how—being moved by that rhythm, being caught up in that pattern—how *shall* we know the dancer from the dance?

MICHAEL GOLDMAN

Fear in the Way:
The Design of Eliot's Drama

"Nothing is more dramatic than a ghost," says Eliot, and his remark offers an illuminating technical insight into every play he wrote. It also has the virtue of forcing us to think specifically about drama, rather than, say, prosody or moral philosophy. Eliot's own practice as a critic and reputation as a poet have tended to concentrate discussion on either the versification and language of his plays or their Christian implications, and this, while leading to much excellent and valuable criticism, has helped promote a serious misunderstanding of his achievement as a dramatist—as a writer, that is, whose texts are designed to allow a group of actors to shape an audience's experience in a theater over a finite interval of time. The possum-like tone Eliot reverts to in discussing most aspects of his dramaturgy other than verse and idiom has encouraged the notion that in matters of dramatic design, particularly the shaping of the action and the use of dramatic convention, Eliot was content to follow the techniques of the commercial theater, and not always the most up-to-date techniques at that. The picture that emerges seems to be of an Eliot laboring to do indifferently what Noel Coward did well, in the hope that verse meditations on the Christian life might somehow be smuggled to an audience while it was being diverted by boulevard entertainment. But if we allow Eliot the benefit of the doubt and approach his plays as the work of a serious dramatist, we can form quite a different impression of their design and of the originality and value of their achievement.

So I turn to the matter of ghosts in order to stress Eliot's art as a dramatist. Attention to the dramatic value of ghosts in his plays will help us see how they are constructed, what precise use they make of the conventions of drawing-room comedy, and why Eliot's achievement in the theater runs considerably deeper than the creation of a mode of dramatic verse.

Drama probably began with ghosts, with prehistoric impersonations intended to transfigure the malice of spirits—to indulge, placate, or wrestle with the dead, to turn Furies into Eumenides. Ghosts are dramatic because they make for action. By their very nature they stimulate that flow of aggression on which all drama depends. Ghosts haunt us—that is, they bring aggression to bear on us in an especially volatile way, a way that penetrates with particular intensity to our psyche and encourages imitation, encourages us to haunt as we are haunted. They are hard to defend against; they cannot easily be subdued or ignored. They create an unstable situation in the external world because their victims must transfer their aggression to new objects. When a real person hits us we can either hit him back or refuse to. Either reaction may make for drama, but the exchange can easily be enclosed, a balance quickly restored. We cannot hit back at a ghost, however, anymore than we can ignore him. The haunting transmits itself through us to a wider world. Thus the classical device of a ghost crying for revenge precipitates the great Elizabethan discoveries as to plot and action—perhaps the greatest discovery being that the ghost could be internalized in the figure of the revenger, who could then be a fully human character—and starring part—while retaining a ghost's peculiar interest and privileges. The ghost makes easy and intense a kind of psychic thrust and counterthrust that connects inner states of feeling—desire, fear, hatred—with movement and change in the external world, the transformation, essential to drama, of activity into action.

A theory of ghosts might make a grand theory of drama, and the historical version of this theory might note that at about the point in time when audiences cease to believe in ghosts they begin to be haunted by memories. People have always had memories, of course, but I would suggest that they are not *haunted* by memories much before Rousseau. In any historical period drama must find its proper ghosts, sources for haunting that an audience can accept as both meaningful and mysterious. Today, for example, we are haunted by unconscious memories as well as conscious ones, and by the past in the form of our parents, our bodies, our economic and social milieu. These are the ghosts that walk the modern stage, many of them, perhaps all, first set walking there by Ibsen.

I sketch this theory of the ghost both to suggest how richly sensitive to the art of the drama Eliot's remark is, and also by way of providing a background for his own ghosts and what he does with them. The structure of each of Eliot's plays is built on a double manifestation of ghosts. At first, the play appears to be haunted by spirits that, though in some respects disconcertingly archaic, still bear a clear relation to our own familiar ghosts—the ghosts we have been accustomed since Ibsen to recognize both in drama and in our lives. Gradually—and this is the fundamental process of Eliot's drama—the ghosts are revealed to be very different from what we took them to be. The original ghosts seem to vanish with an ease that is again disconcerting, but their vanishing proves to be a deeper haunting, more personally directed at the audience. They have turned into other, more persistent, ghosts. The most intense and usually the most effective part of Eliot's drama is not the demonstration that the new ghosts are different, but the manifestation of their true power to haunt—their power to haunt in their true capacity.

Eliot gives his spirits many names. But whether he simply calls them ghosts, as in *The Elder Statesman*, or shadows, furies, spectres, phantoms, spooks, guardians, or even saints and martyrs, it is as ghosts that they perform dramatically. They haunt the characters and inspire the action. Like the Furies in *The Family Reunion* they are often quite explicitly associated with myth or legend, but they also conform to ideas a modern audience can accept. They are ghosts of past associations and deeds, of heredity and environment. The guardians in *The Cocktail Party* may seem enigmatic when considered as guardians of souls, but Reilly is quite familiar to us in his professional role as a guardian of psyches. The ghosts are all versions of the "fear in the way"—the phrase from Ecclesiastes that Eliot used as a working title for *Murder in the Cathedral*—a fear that turns out to be both relevant and irrelevant to the concerns of the characters, and that must be met in the course of the action and either accepted or put aside. In fact, the fear in the way of each play is first to be put aside and then accepted. At the end of each play the false ghosts have disappeared and the true ghosts hover with their honest boredom, and glory over the characters.

Let me very briefly illustrate this by tracing the pattern for each of the plays in turn, from *Murder in the Cathedral* to *The Elder Statesman*. In *Murder in the Cathedral*, the shadows with which Thomas must struggle appear at first to be the Tempters, ghosts of former desires whose enticements to do the wrong thing are quickly dismissed, leaving Thomas to face his real struggle with the temptation to do the right thing for the wrong reason. At the same time there is another spirit in the play haunting the women of Canterbury. It is a fear of Thomas in his capacity as saint and martyr, fear of his coming to Canterbury and of the act of martyrdom to which they are compelled to bear witness. The action of the play demonstrates that this fear is illusory. In one sense the play shows the women are wrong to feel haunted, but in another sense—to which the Knights and the final chorus direct us—the burden of fear and anguish attaching to the figure of St. Thomas remains with them and with us at the end of the play and is indeed revealed only by the play's complete action.

In *The Family Reunion* the pattern is less effectively worked out, but it is simple and clear. The Furies of course begin as Harry's apparent guilt in the death of his wife, the source of his self-loathing and loathing for the human condition. In facing up to them under this aspect, he learns that while their meaning is illusory, they are nevertheless real. They are in fact "bright angels," his Eumenides, whom he must follow. We are left, as in *Murder in the Cathedral*, with a distinctly earthbound chorus burdened by fear and a sense of isolation.

The guardians of *The Cocktail Party* are menacing in a manner that conforms to the prevailing tone of high comedy—they harass Edward with embarrassing questions and surprise visits, they press loathsome concoctions and cryptic advice upon him. It is enough, by Edward's own admission—and this is a point that must be seized in playing—to humiliate him. Their power to humiliate depends of course on the memories and miseries of his relation to Lavinia. Lavinia is described at one point as a phantom; she, brought back from the dead, also haunts Edward as he haunts her. The guardians turn out not to be pests, but, once more, bright angels, yet their power to haunt persists. Most of the complaints Edward and Lavinia bring against each other are disposed of, but their central misery is not. It is Celia who escapes the emptiness and isolation of the ordinary lot, and Edward and Lavinia are left facing both her terrifying example and the absence of transcendent love in their own lives. The mood is hopeful, for their acceptance is a genuine spiritual accomplishment, but a variety of ghosts, of whom Celia must be counted one, haunt the ordinary people who are left behind.

The characters in *The Confidential Clerk* are haunted by disappointments, ghosts of absence—missing children and parents, lost sources of vocation and relatedness. There are also guardian-like figures, Mrs. Guzzard and Eggerson (though lost children haunt them too), whose riddling style imparts a kind of harassment to the persistent memory of these absent spirits, a method similar to that of the guardians in *The Cocktail Party*, who play teasingly upon what is haunting in Edward's and Lavinia's lives. The missing children and parents function as negative bright angels. Their absence seems to leave Sir Claude and Lady Mulhammer, Lucasta Angel, B. Kaghan, and even Colby lacking a meaningful connection with reality. All the missing links are restored in the last act, where Mrs. Guzzard dominates, but the restored relations are in the end far from Eumenidean, except in the case of Colby. The play's focus narrows to Sir Claude, as Colby slips out with Mrs. Guzzard. Mulhammer, shaken and bewildered, is left with Lucasta, whom he has in effect ignored for most of the play. This is his real daughter and he must accept her, as well as accepting all that he does not have. Again we are left with off-stage transcendence and an ordinary figure on-stage facing the loss and insufficiency of ordinary life.

In *The Elder Statesman*, Lord Claverton tells us that Gomez and Mrs. Carghill are ghosts—ghosts of his past, of past crimes. In all the senses announced at the beginning of the play, their power to haunt Claverton turns out to be illusory; the crimes are not real crimes; their threats are insubstantial. But in another sense the ghosts and what they represent are inexpungeable; to face them they must be accepted, for their power to haunt lies in their reflection of the facts of Claverton's own character, which he must accept if he is to cease to be "hollow." For once, the burden is eased for those left on stage. Monica and Charles are brought closer to each other and to Claverton because his confrontation and acceptance of the ghosts has issued in a transforming love. But the discovery, a version of which has been hinted at in the final tableau of *The Confidental Clerk*, depends on clear-eyed acceptance of a haunting loss and limitation.

The great point about the encounter at the end of *The Elder Statesman*, and the great dramatic surprise, is that Claverton does not make his ghosts disappear or render them innocuous by facing them. They continue to be what they always were, and their power for evil is all the more felt for being more fully faced. The price Claverton pays is his son, Michael, but the meaning of the price, as he tells us, is love. If *The Elder Statesman* goes beyond *The Confidential Clerk* by presenting human love as a path to Divine Love, it is significant that the parent-child relation it requires as a dramatic pivot is much grimmer than that between Sir Claude and his daughter. Lucasta is quite clearly a bright angel, as her name suggests. Michael Claverton is not, and he follows Gomez and Carghill.

The pattern I have been describing is suggestive in a number of ways as to the meaning and method of Eliot's drama. What I wish to stress now is its relation to the convention he finally chose to work in—the convention of boulevard entertainment whose fourth-wall realism and bourgeois milieu sustain the workings of a well-made plot. The exact genre may vary with the mood required, but it is always well-made, whether it be the plot of detection, love-intrigue, farce, or melodrama—always the mechanism of secrets to be discovered, obstacles to be overcome, communications to be rechanneled and restored. It will already be clear that the transition from false ghost to true ghost corresponds to the development in every one of Eliot's plays by which the expectations of the convention are subverted. *The Family Reunion* is not an Agatha Christie-like story of crime and punishment but of sin and expiation. The love-tangles of Edward and Celia, Lavinia and Peter, do not lead to complications in the second and third act. Mrs. Guzzard's revelations do not solve the problems carefully established in the first two acts of *The Confidential Clerk*, but show that the problem as it has been stated is irrelevant, and so on. More important, the change in our understanding of the ghosts develops its special meaning and intensity only by virtue of taking place in this type of setting and growing out of this type of dramatic convention.

The well-made play, particularly the drawing-room comedy or mystery, is characterized by an emphasis on mechanical connectedness. The introduction of any significant element implies that this element will be seen to mesh like a gear with all the other elements of the play, and the action of the play will be the operation of all these gears like a single machine. If the key to a letterbox is called attention to in the first act, a significant letter must be unlocked in the last. This sense of mechanical connectedness extends to the society of the play. The characters' lives, pasts, and appetites act upon each other to a degree of intimacy and efficiency that may fairly be taken, in this genre, as an index of the play's success. The result is not always mechanical drama in any pejorative sense, and the connections I am talking about are not always mechanical in the sense that they are superficial or merely physical. But the impression of efficient and causal interconnection prevails, just as it prevails in the various notions of significant action, of cause and effect—of psychological, biological, social, and economic determinism—that drama of this type reflects.

The haunted characters in Eliot's drawing-room plays are pursued by phantoms of connectedness—actions committed in the past, family secrets, old asociations, lovers—the social, sexual, and psychological determinants that are the ghosts of modern drama. But in the end these baleful connections are revealed to be illusory, and the characters are seen to be truly haunted by an inability to connect. The crowded drawing room, the carefully prepared meeting of principals, the statesman's diary are all empty—a cheat and a disappointment. The exact quality of this emptiness is frequently and carefully described—the sudden solitude in a crowded desert, the exacerbated isolation in the midst of an apparent connectedness. It is an isolation that appears inevitable and also miserably unreal because connectedness is felt as the only reality. And here we find the significance of Eliot's convention. This type of isolation cannot be conveyed, for example, on the unlocalized platform of the existential stage, the stage of *Waiting for Godot*. There, isolation represents reality; one is trapped and isolated *in* the real world, the world of one's aloneness, a setting in which the individual, terrified and despairing as he may be, can yet be seen to possess his being. But the sense of isolation from which Eliot's characters suffer—it strikingly resembles that of schizophrenics—is an isolation in unreality. They are trapped in a world of make-believe. In this condition the familiar social world itself is haunting because the very appearance of connectedness only heightens the conviction that one is incapable of connection; one is oneself not real, an empty, worthless, hollow man. The unreal city is oneself and the key confirms the prison.

The dramaturgical point, then, is this. Like the rooms that figure so prominently in *The Waste Land* and the early poems, the drawing room and the dramatic conventions associated with it have a twofold function—they stand for a real world with which the hero is powerless to make contact, and they also stand for the "finite center" of the self in whose unreality the hero is trapped and isolated. In *The Cocktail Party* the isolated cell of the poems has become a modern flat where a man cannot get a moment's privacy, but it confirms a prison still. One achievement of *The Cocktail Party* is its transposition of so much that is haunting in modern life—the horror and boredom and glory that attack and pursue the central sensibility of *The Waste Land*—into the modes of light comedy, but though any production of the play must maintain a proper lightness, it must also be careful not to slight the real pressures that even the most farcical turns of the action apply to the major characters, especially Edward. The first act is a series of humiliations for him, all the more humiliating because they are initiated by the typical raillery and contretemps of drawing-room comedy. And it is exactly this contrast between the convention and his response that allows the play to reveal with lucidity and precision the real sources of humiliation in his life.

Though the later plays are in some respects more profoundly conceived and contain concluding passages of a theatrical beauty quite unique to them, *The Cocktail Party* is still Eliot's most successful play, because in it the vivacity of the author's line-by-line response to his theatrical opportunities is at its height. We feel this most strongly in two ways—first in the interaction of the characters, and second in the use of all the elements in the mise en scène to advance the action and to intensify and render more subtle our experience of it, in particular to heighten our sense that the characters are haunted. In *Poetry and Drama* Eliot complains that too many of *The Cocktail Party*'s characters stand outside the action, but of all his plays it is *The Cocktail Party* whose characters most thoroughly act upon each other in their dialogue. Not surprisingly, *The Cocktail Party* has of all the drawing-room plays the most definite spine, which can be expressed in the phrase *to begin*. From the beginning of the play, when Alex is called upon to begin his story again (the story being drowned, as Julia's soon will be, in the very effort to begin it), until the end, when the bell rings and Lavinia says, "Oh I'm glad. It's begun," the characters are constantly trying to begin and to begin again. And their efforts to begin—if only to leave the room or start a conversation—elaborate the process of haunting and heighten our sense of the fragmentation and isolation of the self that Edward, Lavinia, and Celia experience.

The mise en scène contributes throughout to the sense of an illusory connectedness badgering and isolating the central characters. Take, for example, the strange variety of food that is prepared, consumed, or recommended in the opening scenes. The inadequate tidbits, Alex's culinary fantasies and inedible offerings, the remedies of Norwegian cheese, curry powder, prunes, and alcohol, even the unwanted champagne, all forced upon Edward as he suffers in his constantly interrupted yet unbreakable solitude—these like the genteel disarray of the set, the post-cocktail-party depression (and it has been a badly managed, underfed and underpopulated cocktail party)—like the set, and with a wit and variety that makes the audience alert and sympathetic to nuance, the food plays upon the isolation and debility of the untransfigured individual in the ordinary world. It is a horror and boredom expressed no less exactly than that of the poor women of Canterbury.

All this reinforces the attack Edward undergoes in the course of the first act, the series of humiliations whose insubstantial and amusing surface constantly reminds us how illusory is the ostensibly dense social continuum in which Edward has his being. He cannot be alone for a minute; everyone wants to feed him. He has no privacy; in the nicest way he is interrogated and exposed—but in truth he has nothing but his privacy, and it is a privacy that leaves him with nothing. Left to himself he "moves about restlessly," while the doorbell and the phone keep ringing. Throughout the act, Eliot emphasizes a nagging connection with the outside world by a series of exits and entrances that require Edward to half-leave the stage—to be invisible for an instant, open the door and return with his caller. Edward's world, like drawing-room comedy itself, is a network of insistent social connections which, like his marriage, fail to free him from aloneness and emptiness. In the first scene, he waits his guests and interrupters out, then phones Celia only to receive no answer. The lights go down and come up again. We are immediately aware that no considerable interval has passed; the time elapsed has been pointedly insignificant. Edward sits among the debris as before—potato crisps, glasses, bottles, a forgotten umbrella—playing solitaire.

These examples have all been taken from the first act. Each of the devices referred to—the emphasis on communications, the treatment of food and drink, the behavior of characters when alone—is used in later acts to underline that awareness of transformation which I have argued is essential to Eliot's dramatic technique—awareness that the true nature of the haunting in the play is being revealed. This dramatic imagery is employed with a distinctive wit, a kind of half-explicit mocking of its own recurrence and tendentiousness that sustains the play's tone. Sir Henry's office with its plot-expediting intercom and its carefully scheduled arrangement of exits and entrances contrasts nicely with the nagging persistence of bells and callers in Act One. Similarly, the toasts that are drunk in the course of the play form a sequence that guides our attention from the ordinary to the transcendent. And in the last act we have a cocktail party to contrast with that of the first. The work of the caterers and the new reputation of the Chamberlaynes' parties for good food and drink makes itself felt as a welcome improvement in this ordinary drawing-room world. Even the exits and entrances have been improved—by the presence of a caterer's man who announces the guests. In this world, decent social arrangements still mean much, for they are still the means by which the guardians make their presence known.

As for the behavior of the characters in private, let me take just one example—the moment when Reilly lies down on his couch. In part, this is a joke—a piece of raillery typical of the play but aimed directly at the audience. The couch is one of the indicators by which we have recognized the psychiatrist's office. It has remained empty throughout Reilly's interviews with Edward and Lavinia. Both conventional psychiatry and our conventional dramatic expectations are being mocked. This orchestrates the real shift in expectation, both for us and the characters. The problems of this marriage are not to be located in the usual psychological sources, but in an abiding spiritual deficiency. At the same time the scene marks another transition in the action and in our understanding of the characters. Reilly's moment of exhaustion precedes the entrance of Julia ("Henry, get up") and the interview with Celia; it prepares for our discovery that Reilly does not occupy the highest place in the play's spiritual hierarchy and our dawning sense of what that hierarchy may mean. Again let me stress that the spiritual world is felt as haunting, that it exerts an unsettling and mysterious psychic pressure on the characters. If Reilly's questions and Julia's snooping haunt Edward in the first act, Celia's martyrdom haunts the marital contentment of the last.

The apprehension of a source of haunting and the gradual discovery that the source is very different from what it has been apprehended to be—this pattern of action and feeling is central to Eliot's dramaturgy, and it accounts for an important feature of his dramatic style, or rather for a number of features that together enforce a single theme—that of knowing and not knowing. Take, for example, the motif of the visitor who is both expected and unexpected. The Third and Fourth Tempters both play upon this idea, but it is felt more dramatically in the later plays. Harry is known to be on his way home as *The Family Reunion* opens, but at the point of his first entrance everyone is actively expecting either Arthur or John. Harcourt-Reilly is an unexpected visitor no one is very surprised to see in either the last scene of

Act One or in Act Three of *The Cocktail Party*. The arrivals of Lady Elizabeth in the first act and Mrs. Guzzard in the last act of *The Confidential Clerk*, though carefully prepared and discussed extensively in advance, are disconcerting and unexpected when they happen (and both arrivals are heralded by a series of disconcerting messengers).

Also related to the theme of knowing and not knowing is the motif of the crime that is not a crime. The old man Claverton runs over turns out in the third act to have been dead before the accident. Harry Monchensey did not murder his wife; Lucasta Angel is not Sir Claude Mulhammer's mistress; Edward has not betrayed Celia. In all cases, the revelation is casual, a throwaway defeat of our expectations; it is part of our becoming aware that certain actions and memories do not matter or do not matter for the reasons we thought they did.

Knowing-and-not-knowing is also felt in a recurrent verbal device, prominent as early as *Sweeney Agonistes*—the use of echoing dialogue. This example is from *The Cocktail Party*:

> JULIA: Who is he?
> EDWARD: *I* don't know.
> JULIA: *You* don't know?
> EDWARD: I never saw him before in my life.
> JULIA: But how did he come here?
> EDWARD: *I* don't know.
> JULIA: *You* don't know!

As here, the cadence is usually a mocking or riddling one; we may be tempted to put it down to the Possum-mode of mystification. But the device turns a character's words back on himself, suggesting, as the Fourth Tempter suggests to Thomas, that a man may not know what he thinks he knows, and that we in the audience must expect some change in what we think we know. Our words may be riddles even to ourselves. In the drawing-room plays the echoing dialogue is typically both uncomprehending and disconcerting; it confirms a prison but alerts us to a key.

We know and do not know what it is to act and suffer. How do we come to know more? The answer, given in every play, is: *watch and wait*. But watching and waiting imply a crucial dramatic problem, and the success or failure of each of Eliot's plays may be said to hinge on its solution. At some point in the drawing-room plays, the dramatic convention becomes a fragmented background against which certain characters are seen in a new light, isolated in a freshly haunted world. But this means that there is a risk that the continuity of the action may evaporate, sustained as it has been by the apparent connectedness of the play's world and the now-discredited significance of the ghosts haunting it. At the same time there is the danger that the dramatic interest of the central character may evaporate too. The watching and waiting theme requires that at some moment the hero surrender his role as an agent; he must consent to be passive. He is displaced from a central initiating role to become part of the pattern. The moment of surrender may itself make for a good scene: as when Edward accepts his becoming a thing, an object in the hands of masked actors, or Mulhammer gives up control to Eggerson and Guzzard and absorbs the bewildering results. Claverton struggles with a version of this necessity in his first long speech and again accepts it in the strong scene at the end of his play, and Thomas' surrender is perhaps most powerfully felt in his long cry at the moment of death, which Eliot has considerably expanded from the historical records. But essentially what a character accepts at a moment like this is that he must no longer be a *performer*—and this has awkward implications, both for actor and playwright.

Watching and waiting over any period of time is not very dramatic; it is always a problem for an actor, and Eliot cannot be said always to have solved it. At the very end of *The Elder Statesman*, Claverton says, "In becoming no one, I begin to live," but the actor of this often ungrateful role might fairly complain that, instead of becoming no one, the play limits him to *being* no one for most of its length, that he must watch and wait from the beginning. And in *The Family Reunion*, once the interest of the false ghosts peters out and there is no crime to be uncovered, Eliot can devise no action that engages any of the characters; we are treated to a series of explanations that never become encounters. From *The Cocktail Party* on, Eliot is always able to maintain action and encounter, because the haunting function, both false and true, is taken over by real characters who can make their presence felt in a lively way whenever they appear. Reilly, Julia, Guzzard, Carghill, Gomez—these are good parts, not hard to act. But for the last two plays there remains a difficulty in casting the leading roles which makes it problematical whether *The Confidential Clerk* and *The Elder Statesman* will ever receive performances that can test their best values. In many ways they ask more of their actors than they offer in return. Claverton must be played by an actor not only strong but abnormally unselfish, ready to pass honestly through the long passivity of the early acts in order to contribute to the lovely finale. In *The Confidential Clerk* the problem is even more serious. The characterization of Sir Claude as a financier is extremely flimsy, and his lack of definition as a public figure makes the first act dangerously slack. The deep problem, however, is Colby, whose interest lies far too much in the eyes of his beholders. He must be cast against his part; the role must be filled by an immensely engaging, physically robust actor with no suggestion of priggishness or passivity about him. Here, clearly, the production must make up for weaknesses in the text. Whether we shall ever get such a production, however, remains to be seen.

So far I have been talking mostly about the plays written after *Murder in the Cathedral*, since the subject of ghosts has a special bearing on Eliot's treatment of the drawing-room convention. But my remarks apply to the earlier play as well, for the pattern I have described helps to account for *Murder in the Cathedral*'s dramatic effectiveness and points to meanings that have been overlooked in criticism and production. Let me begin with an objection that is frequently raised against the play: "The determining flaw in *Murder in the Cathedral* is that the imitation of its action is complete at the end of Part One." I do not think this is true to our felt experience of the play, even in a good amateur production, nor to the dramatic intentions clearly indicated in the text.

It is true that by the end of Part One we have seen Thomas accept his martyrdom as part of a pattern to which he must consent for the right reasons, and that we see this acceptance re-enacted both in the sermon and in Part Two, with no modification of theme or deepening of Thomas' response. But the point of the play lies in the re-enactment, since everything is changed *for us* by each re-seeing. The aim of *Murder in the Cathedral* is to make its audience "watch and wait," to "bear witness"—to see the event in several perspectives, each enriching the other, so the pattern may subsist, so the action may be seen as pattern, and so that our own relation to the action, our part of the pattern, may be fully and intensely experienced—and this is not finally accomplished until the very end of the play.

Once more it is a question of knowing and not knowing. Even as the play begins, we know what its climax will be. But by the time we actually see Thomas murdered, after witnessing Part One and the sermon, we see that we knew and did not know. In the same way, the Knights and the Chorus, lacking the knowledge we have, both know and do not know what they are doing and suffering. And of course after the murder, the Knights' speeches show us yet one more aspect of the event that we knew and did not know.

It should be noted at this point that bearing witness, watching the events of the play, is from the first associated both with knowing and not knowing and with fear. In performance we are apt to be unaware of the powerful theatricality of the opening chorus. The theatrical problems of the Women of Canterbury are generally approached by way of voice production and enunciation, and we are grateful—and lucky—if the actresses recruited for the occasion manage to speak clearly and on the beat. Choral acting, as opposed to choral reciting, is usually beyond them. But Eliot understands, as no one except Lorca since the Greeks has understood, that choral writing is writing for the body, and the bodily excitement of the first Chorus derives from the way it joins the feeling of knowing and not knowing to the emotion of fear. The Chorus prefigures the action to come and combines it with a bewildered self-consciousness. We move, they say. We wait. Why do we move and wait as we do? Is it fear, is it the allure of safety, is it even the allure of fear? What kind of fear, what kind of safety? This is exactly the question the play will put about martyrdom, put to Thomas and to us:

> Here let us stand, close by the cathedral. Here let us wait.
> Are we drawn by danger? Is it the knowledge of safety, that draws our feet
> Towards the cathedral? What danger can be
> For us, the poor, the poor women of Canterbury? what tribulation
> With which we are not already familiar? There is no danger
> For us, and there is no safety in the cathedral. Some presage of an act
> Which our eyes are compelled to witness, has forced our feet
> Towards the cathedral. We are forced to bear witness.

The opportunity for the actors is remarkable. The tension between fear and freedom on which the chorus is grounded might fairly be called the root emotion of the theater; it is the same emotion, for instance, that a shaman and his audience share when he begins to impersonate the spirits that are haunting him. The emotion here is intensified through group response, beautifully registered in the language, and profoundly integrated with the action of the play. A crowd of women huddles toward the protection of what it half senses to be a fearful place. The chorus rouses the audience toward the awareness to come, of the church and martyrdom as a painful and difficult shelter.

Thomas is an easier dramatic subject for Eliot than his later heroes, because he remains active all the time he is on stage, aggressive even while he waits and watches. He is supremely connected to this world and the next, secure in his being except for the crisis at the climax of Part One. As far as it bears on Thomas, the pattern of haunting is complete when he says, "Now is my way clear." The true nature of the shadows he must strive with has been revealed to him and he is no longer isolated. We have seen, however, that in the later dramas the pattern of haunting continues to the end of the play and works itself out in the lives of characters for whom such transcendence is not possible. I would like to urge that this pattern is also present in *Murder in the Cathedral*. The sustained pattern of haunting completes the play's design after Thomas' death, and by means of a carefully prepared shift of focus imparts to the whole drama a final richness of impression too easily neglected both in the study and on the stage. As the play finds its structure in our bearing witness to Thomas' martyrdom and, through the Chorus, associates our watching and waiting with a fear that is at times close to panic, so the haunting in the play, the fear in the way of the original title, is finally brought to bear not on Thomas but on the Chorus and on us.

The sequence of events that concludes the play, beginning with the moment the Knights attack Thomas in the cathedral, testifies to Eliot's remarkable control over the resources of his stage. Thomas cries out at length, and the murder continues throughout the entire chorus which begins, "Clear the air! clean the sky!" The stage directions make quite certain of this. The drunken Knights, then, take upwards of three minutes—a very long time on the stage—to hack Thomas to death, while the Chorus chants in terror. Beyond the insistent horror of the act itself there is a further effect of juxtaposition achieved between the murder and the action of the Chorus. Properly acted, the choral text unavoidably suggests that in its terror the Chorus is somehow egging the murderers on, that the continuing blows of the Knights are accomplishing what the violent, physical, heavily accented cries for purgation call for: "Clear the air! clean the sky! wash the wind! take the stone from the stone, take the skin from the arm, take the muscle from the bone, and wash them. Wash the stone, wash the bone, wash the brain, wash the soul, wash them wash them!" The Chorus brings to a flooding climax the ambivalent current of fear that has haunted the Women of Canterbury from the opening scene—attraction toward Thomas and a powerful aversion from him, fear for and of the martyr. The murder is felt not only as a protracted physical horror but as an action in which the Chorus has participated.

The speeches of the Knights that follow are of course sinister as well as comic. The two effects are connected, as Eliot seems well aware, for our laughter involves us, as their fear has involved the Chorus, in aggression toward Thomas. We laugh with release from the constraints of fancy-dress. In the style they adopt, the Knights voice our own impulse to deflate the bubble of archaism, poetry, and saintliness. We share their animus, and their arguments turn the point against us. They have acted in our interests, as de Morville reminds us. "If there is any guilt whatever in the matter you must share it with us."

It is not the confident Third Priest with his dismissal of the Knights as weak, sad men, who has the last word, but the Women of Canterbury, who acknowledge themselves as types of the common man, weak and sad indeed. At the end they dwell upon their fear, which is no less strong for the transcendence they have witnessed. As in all Eliot's plays, the glimpse of transcendence is in itself a source of fear for those who have been left behind. They make the point the Knights have made in argument and that the choral accompaniment of the murder has powerfully enforced:

> That the sin of the world is upon our heads; that the blood of the martyrs
>   and the agony of the saints
> Is upon our heads.

I would suggest that everything that happens in the play from the moment the Knights raise their swords has been designed to give these lines a weight of conviction and a dramatic force that I hope I may by now characterize with some precision—as haunting.

The treatment of the Chorus, then, establishes the pattern Eliot was to maintain in his later drama. And the pattern in turn reflects the originality and strength of his writing for the theater. What Eliot discovered was a way to make drama out of the central subject of his poetry and criticism—the calamitous loss of self and imprisonment in self that haunts our era, a dis-ease that may drive the fortunate man to glimpse transcendence, but which even those glimpses cannot cure:

> The enduring is not a substitute for the transient
> Neither one for the other.
> ("A Note on War Poetry")

The theme pursues Eliot in all his work. In drama, his success was to make the sense of pursuit a ground for action and the theme a source of design, to transmit to his audiences the haunting pressure of "the enduring" on those who, like us, are condemned to roles as actors in a transient world.

DENIS DONOGHUE

Prometheus in Straits: Lawrence and Eliot

But we are all aware that the critical force which holds out against Lawrence, and makes the encounter a classic case in the reception of modern literature, is not Blackmur or Richards but Eliot. It is the juxtaposition of Lawrence and Eliot which demands from us the most sustained response, when we bring to mind not only Eliot's specific comments but the sense of life and the sense of literature which incited them. We have to take the strain of Eliot and Lawrence as presences, for our purpose, equal and opposite. The basic charge which Eliot brings against Lawrence is the charge which Chekhov brought against Dostoevsky: pretentiousness, spiritual immodesty, Eliot called it spiritual pride. 'That dominating, cross-grained and extreme personality,' Eliot called him, 'a man of fitful and profound insights, rather than of ratiocinative powers; and therefore he was an impatient man.' He was impatient, Eliot implied, because he thought that everything depended upon himself; or, in Blackmur's version, because he hardly ever 'saw the use of anything that did not immediately devour his interest, whether in life or in art'. Eliot associated this charge with the 'centrifugal impulse of heresy', set against the orthodoxy which he himself avowed. But the charge can hardly be said to mean much: or rather, it is inadmissible because based as much upon hearsay, lore, gossip, and Middleton Murry's reminiscences of Lawrence as upon the evidence of the novels and stories. Lawrence could defeat the charge by saying that he regards as characteristics what Eliot regards as crimes. But the second charge is more

From *Thieves of Fire*. Copyright © 1973 by Denis Donoghue. Oxford University Press, 1974.

particular, that Lawrence 'wished to go as low as possible in the scale of human consciousness, in order to find something that he could assure himself was *real*'. Put like that, the charge hardly requires an answer: a writer is entitled to go wherever he likes, in the scale of human consciousness, to find what he can register as real. Still, we know what Eliot has in mind; passages in such books as *Mornings in Mexico* and *Etruscan Places*, in which Lawrence seems infatuated with forms of life merely because they come low in the scale of consciousness; like the Hopi snake-dance. But I don't think Lawrence ever proposed that such images should be the end or object of human life; he admired them as a basis for a new beginning, a recourse to the roots of human life, where the gap between nature and culture is small, but still distinguishable. And if a writer proposes to start again, he is well advised to start with the human body and the earth. He will not end there, but his search for subsequent recognitions and more complex stages of development must never lose the sense of their origin.

But Eliot's most vehement quarrel with Lawrence is on the question of morality. In *After Strange Gods* he says that Lawrence's characters 'betray no respect for, or even awareness of, moral obligations, and seem to be unfurnished with even the most commonplace kind of conscience'. It is certainly true of Lawrence's major heroines and heroes that they are not troubled by any official morality of choices and decisions, they act by their own freedom, they are not attentive to laws of church, state, or society. The opposition they recognize comes from the nature of the demand, their own demand for fulfilment; it is intrinsic to their desire, they recognize no other authority. They do not admit, as a critical law to be obeyed, any voice but their own. They demand that their lives be transfigured, and that the miracle take place in terms of their relations to themselves or to others, other men, other women. What such characters ask of each other is that they open the gates upon infinity, the sublime. Since this is an utterly private experience, the question of a moral law is not deemed to arise. These characters do not admit any recognition of society as such, or values arising, with any claim to force, from the fact of community: other people are given about the same attention as the cyclist who comes upon the quarreling Birkin and Ursula in the 'Excurse' chapter of *Women in Love*, they stay quiet for a few seconds until he goes away. The question of conscience is overwhelmed by the consideration of self-determination, self-fulfilment. I am not sure that these charges can be answered. The Eliot of *After Strange Gods* believed that the moral law was absolute, and that it must take precedence over all other considerations, at whatever cost. Lawrence believed that there was no such thing as a moral absolute, and that the fundamental issue was the relation between one person and another, as an extension of the relation between that person and himself.

The only morality his characters acknowledge is the morality of the right relation. In that setting, morality, so far as it is embodied in the promptings of conscience or natural or moral law, is merely an administrative device, no better than any other and no worthier to be obeyed. Success in Lawrence's world means that the characters for whom he cares have brought themselves or brought each other to a satisfactory moment in the action of their lives. Moral questions or considerations which come from outside these relationships do not arise.

Take, for instance, *The Captain's Doll*, one of Lawrence's most convincing stories in the sense that the reader is easily brought to believe in the several characters, their motives and personalities. It is convincing, too, by virtue of Lawrence's remarkable power in securing, on behalf of the characters who deserve such treatment, an impression of their significance as being more than the sum of its appearances. In the case of Captain Hepburn, the reader has no difficulty in registering him as a most formidable presence, a man of continuous if somewhat alien force, even when he is absent from the scene of the story: he is indelible. The question of the relation between Captain Hepburn and Countess zu Rassentlow is the supreme question of the story, and in comparison with that, the relation between the Captain and his wife is secondary, useful only for the light it throws upon the principal relation. The process by which Captain Hepburn and the Countess are at last brought together, after their first meetings and partings, is meant to engage the reader's full concern: he is meant to follow, with full recognition of the issues involved, the subtle alterations of mood and feeling in both characters. The alterations in the Countess's feeling are much greater than in the Captain's; the story implies that he is under no obligation to change, but merely to cause a change in her. The last pages, in which the Countess is brought to change her life and to accept the stern conditions of love which the Captain imposes, are wonderfully done, the reader cannot help but feel the pressure increase, and consign his own feeling to the Captain's power. Much of Lawrence's power is engaged in the Captain's behalf; the reader hardly realises the extent to which he has been affected. It requires a considerable effort on his part to disengage himself from the rhetoric of the story to the extent of recognizing something monstrous as well as something magnificent in the Captain. The reader feels that he is being wilful if he asks, of the relation between the Captain and the Countess at the end, such questions as these: is there any place, in such a relation, for the Captain's two children, cast off in boarding schools? Does the Captain feel at all sad or guilty for the waste of his wife's life, such as it was? Is it entirely obtuse to regard the Captain as a moral gangster?

What I have been saying is merely a gloss on Eliot's critique of

Lawrence, but the strain between the two writers is far more fundamental than the gloss can say. The differences of temper are nearly endless; between Eliot, who secreted poems as if they were the recently discovered work of Language rather than the recently declared work of a man called Eliot: and Lawrence, who consigned everything to the fable of his time, proffering himself as his major work, compounded diversely of choices, chances, works, and days. Eliot could not have written the 'Water-Party' chapter of *Women in Love*; nor could Lawrence have written 'Gerontion', 'Marina', *The Waste Land* or *Four Quartets*. I risk these banal sentences to say something more worthwhile which arises from the comparison: it is essential to Eliot's life as well as to his art that he should say, with full normative intention, 'Humility is endless': it is no less essential to Lawrence's life and art that he would have found the noun in that sentence contemptible. But I must try to go a little further with the comparison, not in the hope of saying anything at all adequate to Eliot's achievement in poetry, but to take the weight of it, in any comparison we might make with Lawrence. Here are the opening lines of 'Burnt Norton', and I choose them as representing not by any means the entire range of Eliot's poetry but the most characteristic of its later directions:

Time present and time past
Are both perhaps present in time future,
And time future contained in time past.
If all time is eternally present
All time is unredeemable.
What might have been is an abstraction
Remaining a perpetual possibility
Only in a world of speculation.
What might have been and what has been
Point to one end, which is always present.
Footfalls echo in the memory
Down the passage which we did not take
Towards the door we never opened
Into the rose-garden. My words echo
Thus, in your mind.
                    But to what purpose
Disturbing the dust on a bowl of rose-leaves
I do not know.
                    Other echoes
Inhabit the garden. Shall we follow?
Quick, said the bird, find them, find them,
Round the corner. Through the first gate,
Into our first world, shall we follow
The deception of the thrush? Into our first world.
There they were, dignified, invisible,
Moving without pressure, over the dead leaves,
In the autumn heat, through the vibrant air,

And the bird called, in response to
The unheard music hidden in the shrubbery,
And the unseen eyebeam crossed, for the roses
Had the look of flowers that are looked at.
There they were as our guests, accepted and accepting.
So we moved, and they, in a formal pattern,
Along the empty alley, into the box circle,
To look down into the drained pool.
Dry the pool, dry concrete, brown edged,
And the pool was filled with water out of sunlight,
And the lotos rose, quietly, quietly,
The surface glittered out of heart of light,
And they were behind us, reflected in the pool.
Then a cloud passed, and the pool was empty.
Go, said the bird, for the leaves were full of children,
Hidden excitedly, containing laughter.
Go, go, go, said the bird: human kind
Cannot bear very much reality.
Time past and time future
What might have been and what has been
Point to one end, which is always present.

It is well known that in the summer of 1934 Eliot visited a ruined mansion in Gloucestershire, and walked in its deserted garden: the house occupied the site of an earlier house which had been burnt two hundred years before. It is a fact only less familiar that Eliot, in an autobiographical lecture in St. Louis in 1959, spoke of another deserted garden which may have meant even more to him than the garden at Burnt Norton. When he was a boy in St. Louis, he lived in a house on Locust Street beside a girls' school called the Mary Institute. The school was founded by the poet's grandfather, the Reverend William Greenleaf Eliot, and it was named after the founder's daughter Mary. From the Eliot home, the schoolgirls could be seen playing next door in the schoolyard, and Eliot recalls that he was allowed to go into the schoolyard, but only when the girls had gone. Once, however, he went into the yard before the last girls had left: he looked in a window, and saw a girl looking out at him, and he fled. So the playground acquired a strange resonance for him, being a place of young girls, echoes, presences, and absences. Clearly, it will not injure the poetry of 'Burnt Norton' if we recite the lore of these gardens, because the passage quoted is in no sense a description of a garden; though I am ready to believe that both gardens played some part in the imaginative process which led to the composition. The passage is not a description, Eliot is not interested in making the reader see the rose-garden, he is using language in such a manner that things are recognized, by its means, rather than seen. The words act 'to compel the recognition they precede'. It is not characteristic of Eliot's poetry, despite *Sweeney Agonistes* and the public-house scene in *The Waste Land*, to make upon an event the demand of immediacy; least of all that kind of immediacy or intensity in which the chief instigation comes from the perceiver's will, and the event is largely an excuse for the release of will-power. The moments of rapture in Eliot's poems are those in which the individual will plays very little part: the soul recognizes the conditions of rapture, but it does not demand them. The only cherished form of intensity is that of recognition, a profound movement of feeling to rise to the occasion. It is never a matter of desire, desire is voided so that the purity of recognition may be complete. The appropriate comparison is with the procedures of Shakespeare's last plays, and especially of that scene which Eliot regarded as the greatest of all recognition scenes in Shakespeare, the restoration of Marina to Pericles. The comparison is valid because the scene gives the intensity of recognition as a process, starting all the way back with Pericles blank and speechless, and going all the way through doubt and faith to the rapture of certainty when Pericles cannot withhold belief and the 'sea of joy' rushes upon him while he hears the music of the spheres. Correspondingly, Eliot's art in the later poems is not a matter of local intensities but of processes of recognition. Facts are given, but given as if their chief privilege were to participate in a particularly subtle music made possible by their humility. Events are presented, but presented as if seen from a distance, so that we see not merely each event but its relation to other events. Words are recited, but as if the chief delight of one word were in leading to the next: they issue from feelings which have detached themselves from anything as rough-and-ready as emotions or desires. Each word serves the pattern, the grand cadence of the passage, directing the reader's mind forward as if to receive, in the fifth Act, another Marina. This kind of poetry is not preoccupied with events as such, but with the relation between palpable sounds and a correspondingly 'unheard' music: the intensity of palpable sounds is not their criterion. In the present passage the unheard music may be received as the music of absence of or 'what might have been', and I find it impossible to distinguish it from Absolute Music, as in Keats's invocation to 'heard melodies' and 'those unheard'. The unseen eyebeam is the visual equivalent of an 'absence in reality', recovered now by memory and association, one vision invoking another. In the organization of the poem, such tokens of rapture are probably nine parts illusion to one part apprehension, and that is the nature of their power. 'What might have been' stands for Absolute Being, and the words register the speaker's sense of it, or the loss of it: it has the same grammatical status as unheard music and unseen eyebeams. The point to make is that in Eliot's later poems what is registered is never that thing merely, or the same thing promoted to vehemence: it is always crossed by another light coming from a long distance, as if its being registered as itself, with whatever force, were not enough. If we approach a rose-garden through passages we do not take and doors we have never opened, the place is an area of feeling as much as an area of horticulture; it is an ablative estate, created as much by feelings of loss and possibility as by the gardener's hand. The first effect is that our response to these words is never allowed to vent itself upon a scene presented for its own sake or with a view to intensity as the main requirement. The words fend us off, as much as they compel our attention; they are a veil through which we are allowed to see, but the veil prevents us from laying rude hands upon the object of vision. The ideal reader is then in the state of consciousness which Eliot certifies in the next passage of 'Burnt Norton':

> The inner freedom from the practical desire,
> The release from action and suffering, release from the inner
> And the outer compulsion, yet surrounded
> By a grace of sense, a white light still and moving,
> *Erhebung* without motion . . .

In that state of consciousness, the words we speak, like the first passage in 'Burnt Norton', have an air of speaking themselves: they issue from a source which does not assert itself beyond the degree of voice or presence.

It will hardly be denied that Eliot, speaking from such a world, was hostile to the Promethean spirit, even in its relatively mild forms. He seems to have thought ofIc Prometheans as barbarians, either in Santayana's sense or in Blackmur's; in the one, the barbarian is 'the man who regards his passions as their own excuse for being', and Santayana had Browning and Whitman in mind; in the other, 'the barbarians are those outside us whom we are tempted to follow when we would escape ourselves', and Blackmur had Whitman and Pound in mind, both 'good poets when we ourselves wish to be fragmentary'. The names do not matter. Eliot even found it possible to rebuke Henry James in this spirit for not toning down 'the absurdities of Roderick's sculpture' in *Roderick Hudson*, 'the pathetic Thirst and the gigantic Adam'. In that novel, James 'too much identifies himself with Rowland, does not see through the solemnity he has created in that character, commits the cardinal sin of failing to "detect" one of his own characters. It is a condition of Lawrence's art that the writer gives his characters as much freedom as they demand, and the benefit of every doubt. Eliot thought him irresponsible, the Prometheanism rampant.

Eliot's critique of Lawrence and of Blake goes far beyond those writers; it presses hard as a principled suspicion upon Promethean motives in general. Indeed, it stands for nearly everything that can be said against Prometheans: a more elaborate prosecution would merely work out Eliot's implications and apply them at large. Of course in the treating of any ostensible 'advance' in the means of culture, it is always possible to present its limitations as radical defects, its accidental qualities as substance: thus Lévi-Strauss in *Tristes tropiques* proposes a relation of cause and effect between the art of alphabetical writing and the exploitation of man by man. By an equally extreme argument, one could say that Prometheus was an interfering busybody, the cause of all our woes, and his gift in poor taste; though it would be impossible to hold that opinion without having accepted the gift and entertained the donor. Such all-or-nothing arguments are beside the point. Even if we take the weight of Eliot's critique, it should not force us beyond the point of looking somewhat ruefully at Promethean motives, and at the bench of desolation from which we survey them. If Prometheus is compromised, it is because his followers have taken to the habit of enjoying their transgression and making of their original sin a deeply cherished illness. Or it is because Zeus has been humiliated, his majesty domesticated. In either of these versions we are moving from epic and tragedy to irony and comedy, as if from *Moby-Dick* to *Pierre*, or from Mann's *Dr. Faustus* to *Felix Krull*. By a turn of the screw, heroes become buffoons and tricksters. But the most probable fate is that heroes and villains are tamed, their violence assimilated to bourgeois norms. This is the fate reserved for them in Ransom's poem, 'Prometheus in Straits'.

Prometheus is presented as surveying the world which he made possible by theft of knowledge: the several stanzas show him visiting the academies, where his beneficiaries are busy with the intellectual pursuits which have established themselves, as for instance a political conference, a class in Art Appreciation, a seminar. Prometheus is displeased: on all sides, he hears talk for the sake of talk, twitterings, exegeses; all the magnificent powers contained in his gift are domesticated, he finds. Zeus is addressed as if he were an Assistant Professor, doubtful about his tenure:

> The prophet is solicited before he has well thundered
> And escapes with credit if he do not turn disciple.

Ransom has always wanted his gods to thunder, and he has rebuked those men, nearly everyone now, who take their gods as images of themselves and find the thunder charming. Religion, history, poetry: each is domesticated, its harm taken away in bourgeois trifles, theories, interpretations, symbols. In the last stanza Prometheus runs away from chattering men who are not really concerned with 'the due distinctions of faith and fact and fiction':

> I will go somewhere by a streamside abounding with granite
> And but little human history and dereliction;
> To the Unknown Man I will raise an altar upon it
> And comfort my knees with bruises of genuflection.

Perhaps Zeus was right, who had in mind letting the human race run out like an obsolete model. In any event, here we have a gently ironic poet bringing the good thief to his knees.

RICHARD ELLMANN

The First Waste Land

Lloyds' most famous bank clerk re-
valued the poetic currency fifty years ago. As Joyce said, *The Waste Land*
ended the idea of poetry for ladies. Whether admired or detested, it became,
like *Lyrical Ballads* in 1798, a traffic signal. Hart Crane's letters, for instance,
testify to his prompt recognition that from that time forward his work must be
to outflank Eliot's poem. Today footnotes do their worst to transform innova-
tions into inevitabilities. After a thousand explanations, *The Waste Land* is no
longer a puzzle poem, except for the puzzle of choosing among the various
solutions. To be penetrable is not, however, to be predictable. The sweep
and strangeness with which Eliot delineated despair resist temptations to
patronize Old Possum as old hat. Particular discontinuities continue to
surprise even if the idea of discontinuous form—to which Eliot never quite
subscribed and which he was to forsake—is now almost as familiar as its sober
counterpart. The compound of regular verse and *vers libre* still wears some of
the effrontery with which in 1922 it flouted both schools. The poem retains
the air of a splendid feat.

Eliot himself was inclined to poohpooh its grandeur. His chiseled
comment, which F. O. Matthiessen quotes, disclaimed any intention of
expressing "the disillusionment of a generation," and said that he did not like
the word "generation" or have a plan to endorse anyone's "illusion of
disillusion." To Theodore Spencer he remarked in humbler mood, "Various
critics have done me the honour to interpret the poem in terms of criticism of
the contemporary world, have considered it, indeed, as an important bit of
social criticism. To me it was only the relief of a personal and wholly
insignificant grouse against life. It is just a piece of rhythmical grumbling."

This statement is prominently displayed by Mrs. Valerie Eliot in her excellent decipherment and elucidation of *The Waste Land* manuscript. If it is more than an expression of her husband's genuine modesty, it appears to imply that he considered his own poem, as he considered *Hamlet*, an inadequate projection of its author's tangled emotions, a Potemkin village rather than a proper objective correlative. Yet no one will wish away the entire civilizations and cities, wars, hordes of people, religions of East and West, and exhibits from many literatures in many languages that lined the Thames in Eliot's ode to dejection. And even if London was only his state of mind at the time, the picture he paints of it is convincing. His remark to Spencer, made after a lapse of years, perhaps catches up another regret, that the poem emphasized his *Groll* at the expense of much else in his nature. It identified him with a sustained severity of tone, with pulpited (though brief) citations of Biblical and Sophoclean anguish, so that he became an Ezekiel or at least a Tiresias. (In the original version John the Divine made a Christian third among the prophets.) While Eliot did not wish to be considered merely a satirist in his earlier verse, he did not welcome either the public assumption that his poetic mantle had become a hairshirt.

In its early version *The Waste Land* was woven out of more kinds of material, and was therefore less grave and less organized. The first two sections had an overall title (each had its own title as well), "He Do the Police in Different Voices," a quotation from *Our Mutual Friend*. Dickens has the widow Higden say to her adopted child, "Sloppy is a beautiful reader of a newspaper. He do the Police in different voices." Among the many voices in the first version, Eliot placed at the very beginning a long, conversational passage describing an evening on the town, starting at "Tom's place" (a rather arch use of his own name), moving on to a brothel, and concluding with a bathetic sunrise:

> First we had a couple of feelers down at Tom's place,
> There was old Tom, boiled to the eyes, blind . . .
> —("I turned up an hour later down at Myrtle's place.
> What d'y' mean, she says, at two o'clock in the morning,
> I'm not in business here for guys like you;
> We've only had a raid last week, I've been warned twice . . .
> So I got out to see the sunrise, and walked home.

This vapid prologue Eliot decided, apparently on his own, to expunge, and went straight into the now familiar beginning of the poem.

Other voices were expunged by Eliot's friend Ezra Pound, who called himself the "sage homme" (male midwife) of the poem. Pound had already published in 1920 his own elegy on a shipwrecked man, *Hugh Selwyn Mauberley*. Except in the title, the hero is unnamed, and like Eliot's protagonist, he is more an observing consciousness than a person, as he moves through salons, esthetic movements, dark thoughts of wartime deaths. But Mauberley's was an esthetic quest, and Eliot deliberately omitted this from his poem in favor of a spiritual one. (He would combine the two later in *Four Quartets*). When Eliot was shown *Mauberley* in manuscript, he had remarked tht the meaning of a section in Part II was not so clear as it might be, and Pound revised it accordingly.

Pound's criticism of *The Waste Land* was not of its meaning; he liked its despair and was indulgent of its neo-Christian hope. He dealt instead with its stylistic adequacy and freshness. For example, there was an extended, unsuccessful imitation of *The Rape of the Lock* at the beginning of "The Fire Sermon." It described the lady Fresca (imported to the waste land from "Gerontion" and one day to be exported to the States for the soft drink trade). Instead of making her toilet like Pope's Belinda, Fresca is going to it, like Joyce's Bloom. Pound warned Eliot that since Pope had done the couplets better, and Joyce the defecation, there was no point in another round. To this shrewd advice we are indebted for the disappearance of such lines as:

> The white-armed Fresca blinks, and yawns, and gapes,
> Aroused from dreams of love and pleasant rapes.
> Electric summons of the busy bell
> Brings brisk Amanda to destroy the spell . . .
> Leaving the bubbling beverage to cool,
> Fresca slips softly to the needful stool,
> Where the pathetic tale of Richardson
> Eases her labour till the deed is done . . .
> This ended, to the steaming bath she moves,
> Her tresses fanned by little flutt'ring Loves;
> Odours, confected by the cunning French,
> Disguise the good old hearty female stench.

The episode of the typist was originally much longer and more laborious:

> A bright kimono wraps her as she sprawls
> In nerveless torpor on the window seat;
> A touch of art is given by the false
> Japanese print, purchased in Oxford Street.

Pound found the décor difficult to believe: "Not in that lodging house?" The stanza was removed. When he read the later stanza,

> —Bestows one final patronising kiss,
> And gropes his way, finding the stairs unlit;
> And at the corner where the stable is,
> Delays only to urinate, and spit,

he warned that the last two lines were "probably over the mark," and Eliot acquiesced by cancelling them.

Pound persuaded Eliot also to omit a number of poems that were for a time intended to be placed between the poem's sections, then at the end of it. One was a renewed thrust at poor Bleistein, drowned now but still haplessly Jewish and luxurious under water:

> Full fathom five your Bleistein lies
> Under the flatfish and the squids.
>
> Graves' Disease in a dead jew's/man's eyes!
> Where the crabs have eat the lids . . .
>
> That is lace that was his nose . . .
>
> Roll him gently side to side,
> See the lips unfold unfold
>
> From the teeth, gold in gold. . . .

Pound urged that this, and several other mortuary poems, did not add anything, either to *The Waste Land* or to Eliot's previous work. He had already written "the longest poem in the English langwidge. Don't try to bust all records by prolonging it three pages further." As a result of this resmithying by *il miglior fabbro*, the poem gained immensely in concentration. Yet Eliot, feeling too solemnized by it, thought of prefixing some humorous doggerel by Pound about its composition. Later, in a more resolute effort to escape the limits set by *The Waste Land*, he wrote *Fragment of an Agon*, and eventually, "somewhere the other side of despair," turned to drama.

Eliot's remark to Spencer calls *The Waste Land* a personal poem. His critical theory was that the artist should seek impersonality, but this was probably intended not so much as a nostrum as an antidote, a means to direct emotion rather than let it spill. His letters indicate that he regarded his poems as consequent upon his experiences. When a woman in Dublin (Mrs. Josephine MacNeill, from whom I heard the account) remarked that Yeats had never really felt anything, Eliot asked in consternation, "How can you say that?" *The Waste Land* compiled many of the nightmarish feelings he had suffered during the seven years from 1914 to 1921, that is, from his coming to England until his temporary collapse.

Thanks to the letters quoted in Mrs. Valerie Eliot's introduction, and to various biographical leaks, the incidents of these years begin to take shape. In 1914 Eliot, then on a traveling fellowship from Harvard, went to study for the summer at Marburg. The outbreak of war obliged him to make his way, in a less leisurely fashion than he had intended, to Oxford. There he worked at his doctoral dissertation on F.H. Bradley's *Appearance and Reality*. The year

1914-1915 proved to be pivotal. He came to three interrelated decisions. The first was to give up the appearance of the philosopher for the reality of the poet, though he equivocated about this by continuing to write reviews for philosophical journals for some time thereafter. The second was to marry, and the third to remain in England. He was helped to all three decisions by Ezra Pound, whom he met in September 1914. Pound had come to England in 1908 and was convinced (though he changed his mind later) that this was the country most congenial to the literary life. He encouraged Eliot to marry and settle, and he read the poems that no one had been willing to publish and pronounced his verdict, that Eliot "has actually trained himself *and* modernized himself *on his own.*" Harriet Monroe, the editor of *Poetry*, must publish them, beginning with "The Love Song of J. Alfred Prufrock." It took Pound some time to bring her to the same view, and it was not until June 1915 that Eliot's first publication took place. This was also the month of his first marriage, on June 26. His wife was Vivien Haigh-Wood, and Eliot remained, like Merlin with another Vivian, under her spell, beset and possessed by her intricacies for fifteen years and more.

What the newlyweds were like is recorded by Bertrand Russell, whom Eliot had known at Harvard. In a letter of July 1915, which he quotes in his *Autobiography*, Russell wrote of dining with them: "I expected her to be terrible, from his mysteriousness; but she was not so bad. She is light, a little vulgar, adventurous, full of life—an artist I think he said, but I should have thought her an actress. He is exquisite and listless; she says she married him to stimulate him, but finds she can't do it. Obviously he married in order to be stimulated. I think she will soon be tired of him. He is ashamed of his marriage, and very grateful if one is kind to her." Vivien was to dabble in painting, fiction, and verse, her mobile aspirations an aspect of her increasing instability.

Eliot's parents did not take well to their son's doings, though they did not, as has been said by Robert Sencourt, cut him off. His father, president of the Hydraulic Press Brick Company of St. Louis, had expected his son to remain a philosopher, and his mother, though a poet herself, did not like the *vers libre* of "Prufrock" any better than the free and easy marriage. To both parents it seemed that bright hopes were being put aside for a vague profession in the company of a vague woman in a country only too distinctly at war. They asked to see the young couple, but Vivien Eliot was frightened by the perils of the crossing, perhaps also by those of the arrival. So Eliot, already feeling "a broken Coriolanus," as Prufrock felt a Hamlet *manqué*, took the ship alone in August for the momentous interview.

His parents urged him to return with his wife to a university career in the States. He refused: he would be a poet, and England provided a better atmosphere in which to write. They urged him not to give up his dissertation when it was so near completion, and to this he consented. He parted on good enough terms to request their financial help when he got back to London, and they sent money to him handsomely, as he acknowledged—not handsomely enough, however, to release him from the necessity of very hard work. He taught for a term at the High Wycombe Grammar School, between Oxford and London, and then for two terms at Highgate Junior School. He completed his dissertation and was booked to sail on April 1, 1916, to take his oral examination at Harvard; when the crossing was cancelled, his academic gestures came to an end. In March 1917 he took the job with Lloyds Bank, in the Colonial and Foreign Department, at which he stuck for eight years.

During the early months of their marriage the Eliots were helped also by Russell, who gave them a room in his flat, an act of benevolence not without complications for all parties. Concerned for his wife's health, and fearful—it may be—that their sexual difficulties (perhaps involving psychic impotence on his part) might be a contributing factor, Eliot sent her off for a two-week holiday with Russell. The philosopher found the couple none the less devoted to each other, but noted in Mrs. Eliot a sporadic impulse to be cruel towards her husband, not with simple but with Dostoevskyan cruelty. "I am every day getting things more right between them," Russell boasted, "but I can't let them alone at present, and of course I myself get very much interested." The Dostoevskyan quality affected his imagery: "She is a person who lives on a knife-edge, and will end as a criminal or a saint—I don't know which yet. She has a perfect capacity for both."

The personal life out of which came Eliot's personal poem now began to be lived in earnest. Vivien Eliot suffered obscurely from nerves, her health was subject to frequent collapses, she complained of neuralgia, of insomnia. Her journal for January 1, 1919, records waking up with migraine, "the worst yet," and staying in bed all day without moving; on September 7, 1919, she records "bad pain in right side, very very nervous." Ezra Pound, who knew her well, was worried that the passage in *The Waste Land,*

> "My nerves are bad to-night. Yes, bad. Stay with me.
> "Speak to me. Why do you never speak? Speak.
> "What are you thinking of? What thinking? What?
> "I never know what you are thinking. Think."

might be too photographic. But Vivien Eliot, who offered her own comments on her husband's verse (and volunteered two excellent lines for the lowlife dialogue in "A Game of Chess") marked the same passage as "Wonderful." She relished the presentation of her symptoms in broken metre. She was less keen, however, on another line from this section, "The ivory men make company between us," and got her husband to remove it. Presumably its implications were too close to the quick of their marital difficulties. The reference may have been to Russell, whose attentions to Vivien were intended to keep the two together. Years afterwards Eliot made a fair copy of *The Waste Land* in his own handwriting, and reinserted the line from memory. (It should now be added to the final text.) But he had implied his feelings six months after his marriage when he wrote in a letter to Conrad Aiken, "I have lived through material for a score of long poems in the last six months."

Russell commented less sympathetically about the Eliots later, "I was fond of them both, and endeavoured to help them in their troubles until I discovered that their troubles were what they enjoyed." Eliot was capable of estimating the situation shrewdly himself. In his poem, "The Death of Saint Narcissus," which *Poetry* was to publish in 1917 and then, probably because he withdrew it as too close to the knuckle, failed to do so, and which he thought for a time of including in *The Waste Land*, Eliot wrote of his introspective saint, "his flesh was in love with the burning arrows. . . . As he embraced them his white skin surrendered itself to the redness of blood, and satisfied him." For Eliot, however, the search for suffering was not contemptible. He was remorseful about his own real or imagined feelings, he was self-sacrificing about hers, he thought that remorse and sacrifice, not to mention affection, had value. In the Grail legends which underlie *The Waste Land*, the Fisher King suffers a Dolorous Stroke that maims him sexually. In Eliot's case the Dolorous Stroke had been marriage. He was helped thereby to the poem's initial clash of images, "April is the cruellest month," as well as to hollow echoes of Spenser's *Prothalamion* ("Sweet Thames, run softly till I end my song"). From the barren winter of his academic labors Eliot had been roused to the barren springtime of his nerve-wracked marriage. His life spread into paradox.

Other events of these years seem reflected in the poem. The war, though scarcely mentioned, exerts pressure. In places the poem may be a covert memorial to Henry Ware Eliot, the unforgiving father of the ill-adventured son. Vivien Eliot's journal records on January 8, 1919, "Cable came saying Tom's father is dead. Had to wait all day till Tom came home and then to tell him. *Most terrible.*" Eliot's first explicit statement of his intention to write a long poem comes in letters written later in this year. The references to "the king my father's death" probably derive as much from this actual death as from *The Tempest*, to which Eliot's notes evasively refer. As for the drowning of the young sailor, whether he is Ferdinand or a Phoenician, the war furnished Eliot with many examples, such as Jean Verdenal, a friend from his Sorbonne days, who was killed in the Dardanelles. (Verdenal has received the posthumous distinction of being called Eliot's lover, but in fact the rumors of homosexuality—not voiced directly in Sencourt's biography but whispered in all its corners—remain unwitnessed.) But the drowning may be as well an extrapolation of Eliot's feeling that he was now fatherless as well as rudderless. The fact that the principal speaker appears in a new guise in the last section, with its imagery of possible resurrection, suggests that the drowning is to be taken symbolically rather than literally, as the end of youth. Eliot was addicted to the portrayal of characters who had missed their chances, become old before they had really been young. So the drowned sailor, like the buried corpse, may be construed as the young Eliot, himself an experienced sailor, shipwrecked in or about *l'an trentièsme de son eage*, like the young Pound in the first part of *Hugh Selwyn Mauberley* or Mauberley himself later in that poem, memorialized only by an oar.

It has been thought that Eliot wrote *The Waste Land* in Switzerland while recovering from a breakdown. But much of it was written earlier, some in 1914 and some, if Conrad Aiken is to be believed, even before. A letter to John Quinn indicates that much of it was on paper in May 1921. The breakdown, or rather, the rest cure, did give Eliot enough time to fit the pieces together and add what was necessary. At the beginning of October 1921 he consulted a prominent neurologist, who advised three months away from remembering "the profit and loss" in Lloyds Bank. When the bank had agreed, Eliot went first to Margate and stayed for a month from October 11. There he reported with relief to Richard Aldington that his "nerves" came not from overwork but from an "aboulie" (Hamlet's and Prufrock's disease) "and emotional derangement which has been a lifelong affliction." But, whatever reassurance this diagnosis afforded, he resolved to consult Dr. Roger Vittoz, a psychiatrist in Lausanne. He rejoined Vivien and on November 18 went with her to Paris. It seems fairly certain that he discussed the poem at that time with Ezra Pound. In Lausanne, where he went by himself, Eliot worked on it and sent revisions to Pound and to Vivien. Some of the letters exchanged between him and Pound survive. By early January 1922 he was back in London, making final corrections. The poem was published in October.

The manuscript had its own history. In gratitude to John Quinn, the New York lawyer and patron of the arts, Eliot presented it to him. Quinn died in 1924, and most of his possessions were sold at auction; some, however, including the manuscript, were inherited by his sister. When the sister died, her daughter put many of Quinn's papers in storage. But in the early 1950's she searched among them and found the manuscript, which she then sold to the Berg Collection of the New York Public Library. The then curator enjoyed exercising seignorial rights over the collection, and kept secret the whereabouts of the manuscript. After his death its existence was divulged, and Valerie Eliot was persuaded to do her knowledgeable edition.

She did so the more readily, perhaps, because her husband had always hoped that the manuscript would turn up as evidence of Pound's critical genius. It is a classic document. No one will deny that it is weaker throughout than the final version. Pound comes off very well indeed; his importance is comparable to that of Louis Bouilhet in the history of composition of *Madame Bovary*. Yeats, who also sought and received Pound's help, described it to Lady Gregory: "To talk over a poem with him is like getting you to put a sentence into dialect. All becomes clear and natural." Pound could not be intimidated by pomposity, even Baudelairean pomposity:

> London, the swarming life you kill and breed,
> Huddled between the concrete and the sky;
> Responsive to the momentary need,
> Vibrates unconscious to its formal destiny.

Next to this he wrote "B-ll-S." (His comments appear in red ink on the printed transcription that is furnished along with photographs of the manuscript.) Pound was equally peremptory about a passage that Eliot seems to have cherished, perhaps because of childhood experiences in sailing. It was the depiction at the beginning of "Death by Water" of a long voyage, a modernizing and americanizing of Ulysses' final voyage as given by Dante, but joined with sailing experiences of Eliot's youth:

> Kingfisher weather, with a light fair breeze,
> Full canvas, and the eight sails drawing well.
> We beat around the cape and laid our course
> From the Dry Salvages to the eastern banks.
> A porpoise snored upon the phosphorescent swell,
> A triton rang the final warning bell
> Astern, and the sea rolled, asleep.

From these lines Pound was willing to spare only

> with a light fair breeze
> We beat around the cape from the Dry Salvages.
> A porpoise snored on the swell.

All the rest was—seamanship and literature. It became clear that the whole passage might as well go, and Eliot asked humbly if he should delete Phlebas as well. But Pound was as eager to preserve the good as to expunge the bad: he insisted that Phlebas stay because of the earlier references to the drowned Phoenician sailor. With equal taste, he made almost no change in the last section of the poem, which Eliot always considered to be the best, perhaps because it led into his subsequent verse. It marked the resumption of almost continuous form.

Eliot did not bow to all his friend's revisions. Pound feared the references to London might sound like Blake, and objected specifically to the lines,

> To where Saint Mary Woolnoth kept the time,
> With a dead sound on the final stroke of nine.

Eliot wisely retained them, only changing "time" to "hours." Next to the passage,

> "You gave me hyacinths first a year ago;
> "They called me the hyacinth girl,"

Pound marked "Marianne," and evidently feared—though Mrs. Eliot's note indicates that he has now forgotten and denies it—that the use of quotation marks would look like an imitation of Marianne Moore. (He had warned Miss Moore of the equivalent danger of sounding like Eliot in a letter of December 16, 1918.) But Eliot, for whom the moment in the Hyacinth garden had obsessional force—it was based on feelings, though not on a specific incident in his own life—made no change.

Essentially Pound could do for Eliot what Eliot could not do for himself. There was some reciprocity, not only in *Mauberley* but in the *Cantos*. When the first three of these appeared in *Poetry* in 1917, Eliot offered criticism which was followed by their being completely altered. It appears, from the revised versions, that he objected to the elaborate windup, and urged a more direct confrontation of the reader and the material. A similar theory is at work in Pound's changes in *The Waste Land*. Chiefly by excision, he enabled Eliot to tighten his form and get "an outline," as he wrote in a complimentary letter of January 24, 1922. The same letter berated himself for "always exuding my deformative secretions in my own stuff..." and for "going into nacre and objets d'art." Yet if this was necessity for Pound, he soon resolved to make a virtue of it, and perhaps partially in reaction in Eliot's form, he studied out means of loosening his own in the *Cantos*. The fragments which Eliot wished to shore and reconstitute Pound was willing to keep unchanged, and instead of mending consciousness, he allowed it to remain "disjunct" and its experiences to remain "intermittent." Fits and starts, "spots and dots," seemed to Pound to render reality much more closely than the outline to which he had helped his friend. He was later to feel that he had gone wrong, and made a botch instead of a work of art. Notwithstanding his doubts, the *Cantos*, with their violent upheaval of sequence and location, stand as a rival eminence to *The Waste Land* in modern verse.

LYNDALL GORDON

Conversion

When Eliot visited Rome in 1926 he suddenly fell on his knees before Michelangelo's *Pietà*, to the surprise of his brother and sister-in-law who were with him. His entry into the Church of England the following year astonished many friends and readers, but for Eliot there was no dramatic change, only 'an expansion or development of interests.' Eliot did not turn from atheism to belief but from spiritual self-reliance to the support of a Church. Eliot in his youth had trusted the inner light, but came to perceive the danger of untempered individualism. The visions of Blake and Yeats, he said, are based 'on the wonders of their own existence'. They enjoy 'a shortcut to the strangeness' without the reality that a Catholic tradition would have ensured. In an essay on the church, which Eliot published in the *Criterion* in 1929, P. E. More grants that private intuition is the essence of religion but finds that insufficient. He admires Whittier's poem, 'The Meeting', which celebrates the holiness of 'naked' experience, without trappings of sacrament or creed, but the experience of the New Englander is too fragile; the private deity fades into 'the flimsiest aura of transcendentalism':

> No, for our growth and sanity in religion we must have something to supply what the inner light will not afford to the isolated souls of men, something to make us conscious of our citizenship in the communion of saints, to supplement our limited intuition with the accumulated wisdom of the race, and in our moral perplexities to fortify the individual conscience with the authority of ancient command.

Eliot's intuition was based on solitude. In his early poetry he repeatedly gives assent to an impulse to withdraw from the world, but at the age of thirty-eight he found a way back through the Church of England whose latitude and tolerance for ordinary sinners provided a corrective to the fanatic edge of his temper. Eliot's youthful imagination came down on the reckless, solitary vigil of Saint Narcissus in the desert; now, in middle age, the Church of England suggested possibilities for saintliness within the parish. The layman must do his saint's work unobtrusively among ordinary people in the home, the bank, the factory or field. The heroes Eliot created after his conversion—the martyred Thomas, the missionary, Harry, his own reminiscing self in *Four Quartets*—work out their salvation at home, among mostly predictable and familiar English scenes.

Churchmen who knew Eliot in later life deny that he was in any way distinguishable from an Englishman born into the Anglican Church. There is no question of superficiality about Eliot's submission to the Church's authority. His confessor, Father Hillier, stressed his unmistakable humility and called him 'a thoroughly converted man'. It is impossible to measure the extraordinary success of Eliot's adaptation to the Anglican community without understanding something of the stubborn self-reliance which he relinquished or controlled.

Eliot's early poetry revives the attitude of the Desert Fathers who, during the century before Rome fell to the barbarians, felt little hope of civilization and retreated into the silence of the desert. For the young Eliot too the highest good depended on an imaginative escape from a corrupt civilization into that haven of silence he first experienced as a student in 1910. The desert idea emerges in 1914 in the figure of Saint Narcissus who is oppressed by a multitude of faces, thighs, and knees, and goes to the desert to become a dancer to God. It recurs in the visionary who persists on his way out of town at the end of 'So through the evening . . .' and in *The Waste Land*'s rejection of the different Voices of society for the sandy road winding among mountains of rock. There is the dead cactus-land of 'The Hollow Men', bleak and threatening, but in 'Ash Wednesday', in a state of genuine penitence, the poet discovers at last 'the blessing of the sand'. He identifies with the prophet, Elijah, who fled to the desert in fear of Jezebel, the avenging queen. Elijah prayed for death under a juniper tree, but was roused by an angel to continue to the mountain where God once made a covenant with the chosen. In 'Ash Wednesday' the exile under the juniper tree wonders if his bones have a right to live, but at that most abject moment he is granted a vision of the promised land: 'This is the land which ye / Shall divide by lot. . . . This is the land. We have our inheritance.'

Despite his solitary nature, Eliot did not find it easy to reject society. There was always the side, distilled in Prufrock, that felt keenly its attractions. In a poem 'Necesse est Perstare?' Vivienne Eliot describes a moment after a literary luncheon when the guests have departed. The wife is thankful for an end to the inane gossip about Clive Bell and Aldous Huxley. She longs to win her husband from his resolve to master London's cultural scene. But he stretches his arms above his head with the weary air of a very old monkey, impervious to her silent plea. In another of Vivienne's sketches she accounts for Eliot's block during 1923 and 1924 by his distracting urge to possess all the kingdoms of this world:

> 'Isn't he wonderful?' whispered Felice. 'He is the most marvellous poet in the *whole world.*'
> 'He might be if he wrote anything,' said Sybilla dryly.
> 'Yes, why *doesn't* he write more?'
> 'Because he wants to be everything at once, I expect. Perhaps the devil took him up into a high mountain and showed him all the kingdoms of the world—unfortunately for him!'
> 'And so, I suppose,' asked Felice naggingly, 'that he doesn't know which kingdom to choose?'
> 'He's still up on the mountain so far as I know. . . .'

Vivienne pounced on the omnivorousness but she did not understand it—that American hunger for experience, knowledge, people, Europe that Henry James presented so sympathetically in a similar image of Milly Theale, poised on a mountain in Europe 'in a state of uplifted and unlimited possession. . . . She was looking down on the kingdoms of the earth. . . . Was she choosing among them, or did she want them all? . . . It would be a question of taking full in the face the whole assault of life, to the general muster of which indeed her face might have directly presented as she sat there on her rock.' But Eliot differed from Milly in his suspicion of the world as a snare. What Vivienne *did* understand was her husband's vulnerability to the devil's temptations.

In some way Eliot was quite alien to the secular mind of his century, as alien as the Desert Fathers had been to the eighteenth-century civic conscience of Gibbon to whom solitaries were deserters from civilization. The monk, Thomas Merton, tried to explain their point of view. Solitaries, he said, regard the world as a wreck and are helpless to do good so long as they flounder among the wreckage. Their first obligation is to find a solid foothold and then to pull others to safety after them. Eliot found his own theological justification in the words of St. John of the Cross which he used as the epigraph to 'Sweeney Agonistes': 'Hence the soul cannot be possessed by the divine union, until it has divested itself of the love of created beings.' It is easy to misunderstand this denial of human love as a sickness of the egotistic imagination but it must be seen in terms of monastic rather than humanitarian or romantic values. Eliot took up a position opposite to the humanitarian attitude of his mother and grandfather that it is through love of one's kind that one approaches love of God. 'I don't think that ordinary human affections are capable of leading us to the love of God', Eliot said, 'but rather that the love of God is capable of informing, intensifying, and elevating our human affections, which otherwise have little to distinguish them from the "natural" affections of animals.' Eliot's early misfortune in his experience of human love perhaps lay behind this monastic conception of divine love as utterly different in kind.

Fantasies of a man's escape from a constraining tie persist in Eliot's works—in 'Elegy', in 'The Death of the Duchess', in 'Sweeney Agonistes' ('Any man might do a girl in'), and in 'The Family Reunion'. Eliot's marital and religious crises were inextricably mixed: through his impulsive love of Vivienne, Eliot made 'that frightful discovery of morality' when 'the not naturally bad but irresponsible and undeveloped nature [is] caught in the consequences of its own action' and 'becomes moral only by becoming damned'. The sense of damnation, the remorse and guilt that Vivienne evoked were essential to Eliot's long purgatorial journey that continued long after his formal conversion and their separation six years later. He could escape her, morally, only by embracing the ascetic Way of the Catholic mystics.

People who met Eliot casually were charmed by his fine manners and modest silence, but those on whose friendship he relied saw a man constantly on the verge of a breakdown, peevish and complaining, oppressed by self-pity, weakened by weariness, and preoccupied with fears of poverty. During 1923 Virginia Woolf was baffled by Eliot's sudden withdrawals from friendship, by his refusal to respond when his shell was prodded, by the laboured perplexities of his rhetoric in which he would enshroud private feelings. One day she, her sister, and husband found him in a state of collapse in his flat. His eyes were blurred, his face ashen, and he could barely stand up to see them out. Eliot wrote to John Quinn: 'I have not even time to go to a dentist or to have my hair cut. . . . I am worn out. I cannot go on.'

Eliot's complaints of poverty—of long hours at the bank that left him exhausted, or huge doctors' bills during Vivienne's bouts of illness—had some foundation, but chiefly they provided a front for other personal problems, moral and domestic, which I think disturbed him more profoundly. Not the grandest stipend, not the pleasantest part-time job could have assuaged Eliot's misery during 1923, 1924, and 1925. Pound and Ottoline Morrell set up separate funds to rescue Eliot for poetry, Virginia Woolf schemed to appoint him a literary editor for the *Nation*, and then all were baffled when he turned their offers down.

The problem, briefly, was Eliot's moral obligation to secure the future for a wife whose health, Eliot told Russell, was now a thousand times worse than when he had married her. For a whole year she had lain in an 'abyss' at 9 Clarence Gate Gardens, 'a helpless and unspeakable wreck of drugs, fear and semi-paralysis'. There was no chance that she would ever manage to shift for herself or endure any privation. And at the very time that Vivienne's needs became so desperate, Eliot first tasted fame and began to feel more strongly than ever the claims of his poetic career. Eliot's friends urged him to leave the bank, but he had to think of Vivienne. He had $2,000 from the *Dial* prize for *The Waste Land*, and could rely on Quinn for substantial gifts. He also had a substantial inheritance from his father, but Henry Ware Eliot, Sr. had disapproved of his son's marriage and had not left the money outright, as to his other children. On Eliot's death the money was to revert to the Eliot family. Until 1923 (when Charlotte Eliot provided for Vivienne in her Will) Vivienne's sole security was Lloyd's Bank, which meant an annual income of £500 and provision for employees' widows, and she insisted that her husband should not leave his job. 'Indeed, if he did take such steps I should bear him a considerable grudge', she wrote to Mary Hutchinson on 4 March 1923. Although she had been one of the first to believe in Eliot as a poet, she refused the traditional demand that a wife sacrifice herself in the cause of genius. She owned to the quite defensible view that it is *not* picturesque to die in a humble cot.

Early in April the crisis broke when Eliot considered leaving the bank without an alternative position and, at the same time, tried to settle Vivienne alone in a cottage near Chichester. Vivienne's colitis took a dangerous turn. Within three weeks she wasted away to a skeleton. She was at the point of death seven or eight times. Eliot, shaken, gave up his plan to leave the bank and fretted over the expense of two specialists from London, the local doctor twice a day, not to speak of the year's rent on a cottage that had proved rather uncomfortable. In a despairing cable and letter to Quinn on 25 and 26 April Eliot said that his affairs were in complete chaos.

The first serious impetus towards the Church of England seems to coincide with the crisis in 1923. It was then that Richard Cobden-Sanderson introduced Eliot to a fellow-American, William Force Stead, who had had himself ordained in the Church of England. Stead drew Eliot's attention to the writings of seventeenth-century Anglicans, in particular those of the Bishop of Winchester, Lancelot Andrewes. Eliot read the sermons on the Incarnation (a notion his Unitarian family would not have stressed). He saturated himself in Andrewes's prose ('but sure there is no joy in the world to the joy of a man saved') and found his examination of the words 'terminating in the ecstasy of assent'. When Eliot first read sermons in 1919 he had been attracted by Donne's spellbinding personality. He now came to prefer the 'pure', 'medieval' temper of Andrewes, who did not stir the emotions so much as stress a settled and resolute will to holiness.

Eliot's entry into the Church was not brought by a ferment that mounted naturally to a point of action. He said that the thought of the intelligent believer 'proceeds by rejection and elimination' until he finds a satisfactory explanation both for the disordered world without and the moral world within. Eliot stressed rational progress rather than emotional states. He accepted the morality of damnation and could not save himself without help. It seems that at this time he felt no religious excitement, and was driven to the Church almost as a last resort.

Eliot first visited an Anglican chapel at Merton College in 1914. (He kept a picture postcard of its interior.) He began to frequent Anglican Churches in the City of London, some time between 1917 and 1921, in search of a quiet spot to think during his lunch hours. At first, he enjoyed the high Anglo-Catholic St. Magnus the Martyr aesthetically, for its 'splendour'; later he appreciated its 'utility' when he came there as a sinner. He was struck, once, by the sight of a number of people on their knees, a posture he had never seen before. Eliot's family was not accustomed to kneel. An aunt, Mrs. Charles W. Eliot, wrote censoriously to a friend who had joined the Episcopalian Church: 'Do you kneel down in church and call yourself a miserable sinner? Neither I nor my family will ever do that!' But Eliot admired this gesture of abasement and worship. Some time during the early 1920s he began to think of the Church not simply as a place where he could find, now and then, some private consolation, but as a way to a new life.

Eliot craved a stronger, more dogmatic theological structure than was to be found in his purely ethical background. Associating his parents' injunctions about 'what is done and not done' with Puritanism, he scribbled on the back of an envelope in about 1923 or 1924: 'There are only 2 things— Puritanism and Catholicism. You are one or the other. You either believe in the reality of *sin* or you don't—*that* is the important moral distinction—not whether you are good or bad. Puritanism does not believe in sin: it merely believes that certain things must not be done.' Eliot's 'Puritan' mother nevertheless prepared the way for his interest in Catholic forms by her own tolerant interest. One of her poems beckons the stranger to the stately Cathedral with its art treasures, its sweet music, and fragrant incense. 'Must not the Lord be near?' she asks. 'Wilt thou not pause to kneel?'

Eliot regretted the cultural impoverishment which he felt resulted from the Reformation. 'Milton's celestial and infernal regions are large but insufficiently furnished apartments filled by heavy conversation,' he said, 'and one remarks about Puritan mythology an historical thinness.' Of all the reformed churches the Church of England retained the closest connection, in formal creed and ritual, with the ancient Roman Church. Eliot, with his interest in a revival of the Catholic tradition, found it freshest in the prayers and sacraments of the Anglo-Catholic inheritors of the Oxford Movement which, a hundred years before, had attempted to revive within the Church of England the best aspects of the Roman Church. For Anglo-Catholics the pulpit was less significant than the sacraments; faith centred on the altar and the confessional which had the advantage of being constant, free from the local limitations of individual pulpits, exempt from the pulpit's competition with mass media, and unimpaired by the fallibility of individual clergymen which had so troubled the learned congregant in 'Mr. Eliot's Sunday Morning Service'. The Anglo-Catholics were a strong and dominant party within the Church at that time and Eliot saw a place for himself there, among people who demanded of themselves a regulated personal life of high sanctity and service.

Why should someone who was not born an Anglican not go directly to Rome? Firstly, Eliot felt that Anglo-Catholicism, unlike Roman-Catholicism, would allow his mind scope. The Anglican Church acknowledges that the truth of the scriptures is only dimly traced and must be verified by individual judgement. The believer takes, at best, only a modest step amidst the encircling fog. Eliot's other consideration was his growing attachment to the English past. His confessor said that he saw his conversion as a return to the religion of the remote English ancestors he recalled in 'East Coker'. Eliot was drawn to the Anglican Church through his historical imagination, associating its creation with the reign of Elizabeth rather than with that of Henry VIII. He used to recall with pleasure its flourishing under Elizabeth and the scholar-clerics who had dignified it in the seventeenth century.

By 1925 it was clear to Eliot that he must make some deliberate change. That year his many anxieties came to a head—another near-fatal illness for Vivienne in the winter of 1924-5, the *Criterion* in danger, and his new collected edition of poems which seemed to him merely an ejection of things he wanted to get out of the way. His anxieties came at him from different areas of his life, but together they urged him to a new resolution, at the end of 1925, to close this unhappy period in his life and begin anew. The stresses of 1925 seem to have been practical ones, but together they encouraged him to change his life in a decisive way. Eliot quoted Orestes saying that furies were hunting him down and he must move on.

His first thought was to leave his wife. By 1925 Eliot was finally convinced that his marriage was doomed. In ten years nothing had really changed—her condition and their relations had only deteriorated. One of Vivienne's unpublished sketches provides an almost diabolically detached report of a husband's miserable homecomings from work. 'Anthony' comes in very quietly and hangs about in the hall for a minute, dreading his wife. 'There were many things he dreaded. That Ellison might have a headache, that she might be irritable and hate him, that she might be in despair or have with her her greatest friend who would have been quarrelling with her.' He moves almost stealthily to his study, hoping it will be empty, to find his wife lying in wait on the sofa. Vivienne's moods and nervous states must have given her husband ample cause for self-pity, but I think their marriage was also blighted by something else, something in Eliot, that he half-recognized as the underlying cause of their troubles. What exactly it was, one can only conjecture from other fragmentary remarks in his poems and in Vivienne's sketches. He seemed to suffer from an inability to empathize with suffering outside his own experience. In a strange guilty poem he published in 1924 he said he could see eyes in a golden vision, but not eyes in actual life, in tears. The latter he saw only through a blank, almost sealed-off division. 'This is my affliction', he repeated, 'This is my affliction'.

There is another picture of Eliot's curious detachment in a sketch by Vivienne called 'Fête Galante'. At a bohemian party, a lively girl called Sybilla encounters an American financier-poet. She describes him leaning with exaggerated grace against the fireplace, refusing to speak. Her portrait is rather like the one painted by Wyndham Lewis of T.S. Eliot a few years later—a heavy, slumbering, white face; long hooded eyes, unseeing and leaden-heavy; a large sleek head. She is fascinated, but recognizes that there is something strange about him. 'I like him, I like him', she muses, '—if only he would—What? What is wrong, what missing?'

If there is any truth in this sketch it is not surprising that Vivienne should have had a hopeless sense of exclusion. 'Sybilla' is Eliot's Sybil in the epigraph to *The Waste Land*. She who had directed Aeneas to the Underworld now withers eternally in a cage. There is a pathetic description of Vivienne Eliot in 1923, a convalescent—heavily powdered, shaky, and somewhat overdressed—being driven into the country to enjoy Sunday afternoon tea with the Woolfs, where her husband pressed her to take medicine and Virginia lightly snubbed her small effort at conversation. In the winter of 1924-5 she was struck down by a terribly painful illness just as she had begun, at last, to show signs of new morale. All through 1924 she had been writing and publishing anonymously in the *Criterion*. In her husband's opinion she wrote 'EXTREMELY well' and with 'great originality'. Her sketches of a dingy Parisian hotel and its inhabitants, a *thé dansant* in London, or a boring bohemian party where ballet dancers are shepherded in by a 'macaw', are all emotionally alive and critically observant, with a clever choice of detail reminiscent of Katherine Mansfield.

In 1925 Eliot wrote to Russell that the obvious alternative to their present life was that they should part—if only Vivienne could manage to live on her own. It is interesting that he did not complain of her illnesses but of the damaging relationship. He blamed partly himself—'living with me has done her so much damage'—and partly her emotional immaturity. 'I find her still perpetually baffling and deceptive', he wrote. 'She seems to me like a child of 6 with an immensely clever and precocious mind. . . . And I can never escape from the spell of her persuasive (even coercive) gift of argument.' In 1927, no longer quite normal, she went to a centre for nervous disorders at Divonne-les-Bains, near Geneva. A fellow-patient has recorded vividly his first sight of Vivienne 'as she walked almost as though in a trance along the wooded path. Her black hair was dank, her white face blotched—owing, no doubt, to the excess of bromide she had been taking. Her dark dress hung loosely over her frail form; her expression was both vague and acutely sad.'

In the end Eliot did not leave his wife until 1933, but he made several other attempts to change his life. He went to beg help from Geoffrey Faber, who agreed to take him into his new publishing firm in the autumn of 1925; here he found work that was closer than banking to his literary interests. There is a photograph of Eliot in Bloomsbury in 1926 in his new role of elegant young publisher: his bowler hat very straight, he leans casually on his tightly-rolled umbrella. He also moved to a pleasanter neighbourhood, 57 Chester Terrace in S.W. 1. Then in 1927 he joined the Church of England and, in November, exchanged American for British nationality.

In 1914 Eliot might have become a Christian in a mood of passionate assent; by 1927 he had hesitated too long for such a mood to be possible. What he needed now was essentially a haven from the turmoil of 'heaven and damnation / Which flesh cannot endure.' Forced to mute his longing for religious extravagance (because 'these wings are no longer wings to fly'), hoping no longer to recover the 'infirm glory' of private intuition, 'the one veritable transitory power' of his youth, he now aspired only to keep his soul alive by regular prayer. In 1926 he began to attend regularly at early-morning Communion. He learnt the morality of patience ('teach us to sit still') and that 'humility is the beginning of anything spiritually or even culturally worthwhile'. In the years immediately preceding his conversion Eliot no longer sought the visionary 'silence' of his youth, nor waited, like Gerontion, for the heavens to open, but began to think of religion as a long-term regimen. Under the influence of Bishop Andrewes and St. John of the Cross he moved away from his mother's revelatory moment of 'truth' towards more moderate goals of 'prayer, observance, discipline, thought and action.'

On 13 November 1926 Eliot asked Stead if he might be confirmed in the Church of England. He wished for absolute secrecy; he hated, he said, dramatic public conversions. As a Unitarian, Eliot had never been baptized in the name of the Trinity, so Stead arranged for his baptism in his own village of Finstock, in the Cotswolds. Eliot's godfathers were to be B.H. Streeter, a theologian of Queen's College, Oxford, who did much to recommend the Church to educated agnostics, and Vere Somerset, a historian, a fellow of Worcester (the college with which Stead was associated). On 29 June 1927 the doors of Finstock Church were firmly locked against idle spectators, and Stead poured the waters of regeneration over Eliot's head.

Next morning Eliot was taken to the Bishop of Oxford, Thomas Banks Strong, at Cuddesdon. In his private chapel the Bishop laid his hands on Eliot's head and said: 'Defend, O Lord, this thy Servant with thy heavenly grace, that he may continue thine forever.'

The third, and for Eliot probably the most important, ceremony only came nine months later when he made the first confession, in about March 1928, after finding a spiritual director in Father Underhill. Eliot said that 'the recognition of the reality of Sin is a New Life'. All his adult life he had been haunted by a sense of guilt—most frequently, judging by his poems, sexual guilt and withdrawal of self—which now found relief. Eliot wrote to Stead of his extraordinary sense of surrender and gain, as if he had finally crossed a very wide, deep river, never to return. He liked Underhill but sometimes felt he needed the severer disciplines of a priest called Whitby. He wanted something more ascetic, more violent, more 'Ignatian'. One of his first tasks was to come to terms with celibacy and find it easy for the first time. In his poem, 'Animula', he speaks of 'denying the importunity of the blood' and living solely for 'the silence' after the blessing.

Eliot's penitent in 'Ash Wednesday', turning and turning on the winding stair, acts out the two mental 'turns' Andrewes prescribed for a conversion: a turn that looks forward to God and a turn that looks backward to one's sins, sentencing oneself for the past. In this sermon 'Of Repentance', preached on Ash Wednesday, 1619, Andrewes gives an exhaustive analysis of the demands which conversion must make on the most developed and sensitive conscience—the weighing of motives, the 'hatred of sinne', the guard against hypocrisy.

There is always a public and a private side to conversion. Eliot was impatient to fix his identity and be made wonderfully anew. He announced his conversion as an achieved goal much as the American Puritans would give public testimony of faith before being received into the communion of saints. As a public figure in the thirties he took it upon himself to call for the religious reform of society at school prizegivings and church conclaves. The private self lagged behind. In 'Ash Wednesday' and the Ariel poems, written between 1927 and 1931, Eliot wonders if he does not belong with those who espouse

Christianity officially without being properly committed, whose ostentatious piety is 'tainted with a self-conceit', who 'are terrified and cannot surrender', and who 'affirm before the world and deny between the rocks'.

Eliot did not make it easy for his contemporaries to understand his conversion. In 1928 he announced rather curtly that he was an 'Anglo-Catholic in religion'. It sounded oddly wilful and insistent and, furthermore, was coupled with dogmatic beliefs in royalism and classicism. Eliot rashly gave the impression that all these beliefs were of equal importance to him. He did not make it clear that his royalism and classicism were subsidiary to his Christianity and should be taken in a special way. By royalism Eliot did not mean George V or any living ruler but an ideal similar to Sir Thomas Elyot's, a hope that the majesty, propriety, and responsibility of an ideal ruler would reform people from above. He believed, like Maurras, that church and king should work together. The king, he said later, 'had not merely a civil but a religious obligation toward his people'. Similarly, Eliot invoked classicism to uphold a Christian education. 'If Christianity is not to survive', he wrote, 'I shall not mind if the texts of Latin and Greek languages become more obscure and forgotten than those of the language of the Etruscans.'

It seemed to many of Eliot's contemporaries that he wilfully averted his eyes from social problems between the wars and took refuge in obsolete institutions. *TLS* called Eliot a kind of traitor. Edmund Wilson deplored 'the unpromising character' of the ideals and institutions he invoked and the 'reactionary point of view'. The *Manchester Guardian* said that only an American expatriate could go so far in the direction of the right.

These critics were baffled because, perhaps naturally, they assumed Eliot was allying himself to an institution whose mass appeal was rather weak between the two wars. But for Eliot belief was 'something detached from the temporal weakness or the corruption of an institution'. Like many religious thinkers he put together a faith which answered private needs and then attached that to an institution which he believed to carry the living stream of Christianity but which needed reform. Eliot's attachment to Anglicanism had this dual aspect. He saw means of support and self-correction within the English traditions; at the same time he brought something of himself to the Anglican Church, a spirit more vehement, more dogmatic and zealous. As Newman remarked: 'It is not at all easy . . . to wind up an Englishman to a dogmatic level.' The average layman was more concerned with the demeanour of the vicar than with theology and reform. Eliot's dogmatic orthodoxy, his concern with damnation, his intolerance in his earlier years for ordinary sinners, his sense of civilization's decay and doom, his intuitions of a 'promised land beyond the waste'—all this suggests a lingering Puritan strain, rather different from the equable, mild-mannered temper of the gentlemen-clergymen with whom Eliot began to associate and to whose habits he wholly conformed.

Eliot's temperament craved an exacting moral code. Chastity, austerity, humility, and sanctity, he said he must have—or perish. This code did not, of course, conflict with the aims of Anglo-Catholics, but it was *sui generis*. To express his ideals of virtue Eliot fastened on an English institution that was particularly mild in its minimal demands and set about reforming it from within. During the thirties he called upon Anglicans for a stricter theology, for discipline and asceticism, for a religion not 'watered down and robbed of the severity of its demands'.

A tireless Calvinist, Robert Lowell called Eliot, who harried his pagan English public with godliness and austerity. The English perhaps served Eliot as the lost tribes, as the Indians had served the religious energies of the Puritans and as the Westerner had served the missionary zeal of Eliot's grandfather in mid-nineteenth-century St. Louis and his uncle in late-nineteenth-century Oregon. Lowell recognized in Eliot's attraction to Anglicanism the authentic colour of the New Englander who would preach a more rigorous code than that which prevailed and enjoy its proprieties of form and the introspective mood it induced. If Eliot's mask suggested England, his inbent eye recalled the New England divines.

Eliot's public was, I think, partially justified in its unfriendly reaction to his faith. He had misled it by defamiliarizing the message of *The Waste Land* and then baffled it by his odd attachment to the Anglican Church. The hostility Eliot evoked, however, seems excessive and probably lay outside Eliot personally, in the age itself. Edmund Wilson deplored the forced mating of New England temper with the Anglican mode, yet admitted at the same time the unfriendliness of their age to anything religious.

Eliot joined a church which, for him, retained the façade of the Elizabethan Establishment, a national church reinforced by secular power. Beside support for his private life, he found strength also in a sense of community and tradition. Living communities in America are based less on natural ties of kinship and familiarity as on a shared theory. Whether the group be based on religious belief, a political platform, or an academic field, there will be a strong emphasis on creed and jargon, a strictness within the ranks combined with a fair degree of intolerance for the uninitiated. To a non-American such groups will hardly seem communities because of the impermanence of personal and local ties. The members share no past and, very likely, no future. All they have in common—and this they will insist on—is the label. Eliot pinned on his Anglican label in the preface to *For Lancelot Andrewes*. He brought to the Church of England the American's capacity to commit himself to an idea with a fervour that seems at once strained and brave, wilful and yet attractive in its sheer vitality of moral passion. Yet in his thorough and permanent identification with the English past and locale in 'East Coker' and 'Little Gidding', which celebrate communities based on family ties, and in his acceptance of pastoral responsibility in *The Idea of a Christian Society*, Eliot became more genuinely English than any American before him.

Eliot's attachment to Anglicanism may be justified from an ideological as well as a personal angle. He discarded popular ideologies of social change—extremist politics and liberal optimism—as solutions to cultural despair, and offered as an alternative the idea of a community knit together by religious discipline. Liberal humanism, Eliot felt, could work only for a few highly-developed individuals who lived in the aftermath of a strong religious tradition. Babbitt's doctrine of the 'inner check' was too subtle and private to be the masses' alternative to the encroaching chaos of the thirties. Men like Russell and the Huxleys, who believed in a civilized but non-religious mentality, had too naïve expectations of human nature. Eliot was not against liberalism or democracy *per se*; he simply feared that they would not work: 'It is not that the world of separate individuals of the liberal democrat is undesirable', he wrote, 'it is simply that this world does not exist.' Eliot saw the masses, with their illusion of freedom, manipulated by a society organized for profit which would influence them by any means except their intelligence. He thought that unless there was an ideal that could comprehend all of life, namely Christianity, the masses would find the burden of thought, each man alone, so difficult that they would come to crave simplified monistic solutions, like the racist solution of Nazi Germany.

Eliot saw in the English Church decency, common sense, and a capacity for compromise that, he felt, might provide a proper corrective to the faddist modern mind. He deplored the kind of lazy, facile mind that advocated ruthless reforms and leapt across all existing reality to some utopian ideal—through fascism or communism—what he called 'the gospels of this world'. In 1910 already, Gide had prophesied that the weakness of the twentieth-century mind would be in 'locating the ideal of perfection, not in equilibrium and the middle path, but in the extreme and exaggeration'. Eliot thought he found a responsible and rational answer in the *via media* of Elizabethan Anglicanism and praised its talent for compromise, its moderation and flexibility. 'In a period of debility like our own,' he wrote, 'few men have the energy to follow the middle way in government; for lazy or tired minds there is only extremity or apathy, dictatorship or communism, with enthusiasm or indifference.'

In the thirties Eliot was criticized for his refusal to turn the *Criterion* into a forum for writers with radical social ideas. It seemed to many that he

was simply aligning himself with a crass, old-fashioned conservatism. Although Eliot did discount the sweeping ideologies for social change then
current, his own 'scheme for the reformation of society' was not old-
fashioned. He saw that the future lay with the lower middle class, who would
be the most numerous and whose taste would be indulged. He assumed that
the lower middle class would have inferior taste, but he did not kick against
this. Instead he proposed a reformation of society set at a low level: 'a social
minimum', he called it. There would be rural communities where Christian
values would not be fervently upheld but would be assimilated into humdrum
lives as mere behaviour and habit. He proposed communities small enough to
consist of a network of direct personal relationships, so that people would
watch over one another. He felt that a renewed sense of community would
energize society, although he admitted that the rural ideal did not fit very well
into the twentieth-century urban-industrial scene. Eliot also felt there should
be a place for a spiritual élite, not to command or compel other people, but
to preserve the best standards of thought, conduct, and taste so that people
should have a sense of higher forms of life towards which they might, if they so
wished, aspire.

It has not been customary to take much notice of Eliot's ideological
position, yet it seems, from a historical distance, far more reasonable than the
sweeping ideologies fashionable in his day. His modest ideal was men's virtue
and well-being in community for all, and for a few, the divine beatitude. He
wanted a community that would enrich the individual's sense of dignity, and
he was indifferent to twentieth-century social schemes in which the individual was of small worth. Only one or two recognized the reasonableness of
Eliot's position. In 1940 Lionel Trilling wrote that, although Eliot might have
deceived himself in considering the Church an effective force for social
reform, he had provided one moderate answer that favoured morality and
human dignity, rare in his time.

The difficulty in studying Eliot's life lies not in his religious search,
which seems quite straightforward, but in isolating what was innovative and
original in his vision of the world from what was idiosyncratic and sometimes
distorted. William James pointed out how each temperament makes religion
according to its needs. If one is humane, one's religion tends to be comforting; if one is self-absorbed and obsessed with a darker life, one's religion tends
to exalt self-sacrifice and drastic cures. Eliot braced himself for 'cords and
scourges and lamentation' and 'a whole Thibet of broken stones / That lie,
fang up, a lifetime's march.' His nature, like that of his early hero, the
martyred Saint Narcissus, was drawn by Christianity's martyrdoms and feats
of asceticism rather than by its more compassionate humane goals. He
certainly knew, after his conversion, moments of singing happiness, recorded

in the lyrical parts of 'Ash Wednesday' and 'Marina'; he may, late in life, have discovered the comforting face of religion, but most of his life was spent in the shadow of its torments rather than its blessings.

Eliot was sensitive to the power of evil in human hearts and felt that his conception of sin, in a twentieth-century world dedicated to material, political, and sexual cures, was itself a triumph. He felt the devil not so much in social wrongs, but within, and believed that the chief purpose of civilization was to cope with the notion of original sin. This defensible point of view found an unhappy focus in Eliot's routine identification of women with sin. He regarded lust as the most corrupting of all sins and, as a young man, he wished the flesh could be denied, burnt away by that refining fire he so often invoked. Soon after his conversion he wrote savagely that those who 'suffer the ecstasy of the animals' may look forward only to death.

Eliot always acknowledged and derided the idiosyncratic element in his philosophy. Although he presented himself as an exemplary figure, he frankly included his personal flaws. Eliot had an extraordinary drive for perfection, and in his early years hunted for signs that he had been singled out in a special way. He wished to be God's ambassador, but admitted again and again in his early years that he could not honestly claim the credentials. Even in his light-filled moments he retained a degree of modesty or hesitation. Because of his distance from God—a distance reinforced by his times—the approach had to be willed, doggedly and alone. Eliot's mental isolation perhaps brewed the eccentric elements in his early life—the distrust of women and the narrow self-absorption. Eliot's personality was self-centred enough to assume that the world and its vicissitudes—its women, its wars, seasons, crowds—existed as signals for his private conduct. The isolation and the absence of signs, of which Eliot complained in 'Gerontion', brewed also a certain wilfulness. Eliot's poetic record did not concentrate on the beatific vision but on himself, his determination to be recognized and chosen.

Eliot passed his youth walled-in by shyness and vast ambition. His adult life may be seen as a series of adventures from the citadel of his self in search of some great defining experience. He made expeditions across a perilous gap that divided him from the great world, and ventured into society, into marriage, into religious communion. He tried to maintain the polite, even curiosity of an explorer far from home, but each time had to withdraw—shuddering from the contact—to his citadel, where he would then labour to record, as precisely as possible, his strange encounters. It was soon apparent to Eliot that the religious encounter was the most commanding of his experiences but, ironically, with this perception the gap seemed to widen, to become ever more difficult to cross. By 1925, it had become clear to him that if he were to cross the gap successfully he would have to abandon his citadel, and plunge into a journey of no return. The plunge came with his first confession in 1928; during the thirties he adapted to living in an Anglican clergyhouse; at last, with the genuine state of self-abnegation recorded in *Four Quartets*, came the chance to commune with God on Little Gidding's holy ground.

At each stage of his career Eliot defined his identity and measured his distance from enlightenment. There was, in his poetry, a persistent self-portraiture—from the languid, well-dressed gentleman in 'Spleen', who waited impatiently on the doorstep of the Absolute, to Prufrock, whose impulse to assault the universe with a prophetic truth beat beneath his anxiously correct façade; and from the phantom pilgrim searching the city for a miraculous cure for depression to the anxious penitent patiently climbing the purgatorial stair. One developing personality redefined, in each poem, the position won in the previous poem. From the start, Eliot was preoccupied with his own special fate, but he was uncertain how to characterize himself. He sensed his identity as a 'shadow of its own shadows, spectre in its own gloom'. Eliot haunted his poems like an irresolute ghost seeking shape and form and visible role. When at length he was sure of his best self, he suddenly revealed a preacher, his outlines distinct, his feet firmly planted on an Anglican platform.

One of the persistent features of Eliot's early years is his displacement in his time. He derided his contemporaries' faddist political solutions, their smug rationalism, their meaningless toys—horoscopes and porcelain collections—their boring stereotyped parties, their magazine-styled romances. Eliot saw the children of the early twentieth century as an alien people clutching cheap gods. Like a prophet he denounced those who sat 'in the sty of contentment', and those who glittered 'with the glory of the hummingbird' and, above all, those who supported a predatory commercial society. He had seen in his youth in America the hypertrophy of the motive of profit as a public ideal and the gross misuse of money. In 1939 he foresaw that these evils were more tenacious than those that provoked the Second World War. In 1939 his rhetoric seemed irrelevant; several decades later his denunciations seem pertinent:

> Surely there is something wrong in our attitude towards money. The acquisitive, rather than the creative and spiritual instincts, are encouraged. The fact that money is always forthcoming for the purpose of making more money, whilst it is so difficult to obtain . . . for the needs of the most needy, is disturbing to those who are not economists. I am by no means sure that it is right for me to improve my income by investing in the shares of a company, making I know not what, operating perhaps thousands of miles away, and in control of which I have no effective voice.
>
> (Postscript, *ICS*)

He also criticized the exhaustion of natural resources by unregulated industries ('exploiting the seas and developing mountains') and warned that 'a good deal of our material progress is a progress for which succeeding generations may have to pay dearly. . . . For a long enough time we have believed in nothing but the values arising in a mechanized, commercialized, urbanized way of life: it would be as well for us to face the permanent conditions upon which God allows us to live upon this planet.'

Eliot had little hope that a civilization smugly assembled on congeries of banks, industries, and insurance companies, would listen to his exhortations. He wrote that God commanded him to 'prophesy to the wind, to the wind only for only / The wind will listen.'

Eliot wilfully adopted roles unlikely to charm the audience of his day, of pilgrim and preacher. The models of manhood by which he measured himself—Augustine, Lazarus, Ezekiel, Elijah, Parzival—were heroes of other, more religious ages. The cultural anecdotes in *The Waste Land* temporarily deluded Eliot's postwar audience into adopting him as a child of their times. The 'lost' generation followed him willingly to the brink of cultural despair, but wondered at his inclinations when he went beyond it. He ventured alone in search of the lost ideals of religious communities, and occasionally bethought himself of his generation and called back urgent exhortations. These sounded odd in their ears—dogmatic, wilful, and irrelevant.

Through his personal record Eliot tried to give back to the early twentieth century a world in which men lived by fresh visions and to restore the moral dimensions of a universe in which visions belonged. Eliot himself enjoyed only infrequent, and often frustrating, moments of revelation—the silence between the waves, the silence in the streets of Boston, the ring of silence in the Parisian attic—but these were sufficient to initiate in him a new sense of the meaning of life. He used to experience a vision not as pleasure but as a sudden relief from an intolerable burden. It was as if strong habitual barriers were broken down. 'Some obstruction is momentarily whisked away', he said. Although the vision commanded Eliot's life and dictated his message, he tended, in his published poetry, to gloss over it and to concentrate on the doubts and struggles that followed. These were easy to communicate, while the vision, he realized, was essentially incommunicable. The habitual barriers re-formed very fast.

Eliot showed great courage and persistence in defending his faith as an inescapable human need and in pointing out that what was objectionable to one generation was simply what it was not used to. After moving in intellectual circles he experienced, in his identification with the church, an odd but exhilarating feeling of intellectual isolation. When he was presented with the Emerson-Thoreau medal, in 1959, he was called the spiritual heir to a line of 'come-outers', New Englanders who spoke out for their private convictions, who braved misunderstanding, and welcomed the solitude of original insight. Eliot set himself to rediscover modes of experience absent from the world into which he was born: the saintly life, the Christian community, religious fear and hope. If he could not quite live the saintly life himself, if he could not speak directly to his contemporaries, he still hoped his story would benefit generations to come, 'in a world of time beyond me'. He consigned his deeds to oblivion, but proffered his love to the choice souls of the future, 'the posterity of the desert'. In 'Song for Simeon' he hoped that they would acknowledge and re-enact, with greater success, his lonely watch. They would praise God and suffer derision and discover light upon light, mounting the saints' stair.

RUTH NEVO

The Waste Land:
Ur-Text of Deconstruction

I have no pretensions to being a deconstructionist in any sense which would imply membership in that august company, so far as it is a company. I simply count myself fortunate in having younger colleagues, friends, and students willing to keep me up to date and initiate me into the perceptions and perspectives of a movement in criticism exciting enough to have discombobulated my own entrenchedly old-fashioned New Critical habits of mind. I believe it to be, as it has developed over the last ten or fifteen years, the most fruitful, stimulating, and revivifying of the intellectual shifts so constantly taking place around us. Voices (not necessarily the implied author's, mind you—that eminent personage has been dethroned—but real voices) are once again to be heard in literature, which methodological ossification had begun to turn into magnificent museum pieces. And not only is it humane and humanizing in this way but also democratic and emancipatory. What Robert Crosman has called "imperial truth"—the monistic, single, all-encompassing, unified meaning supposed to reside in the articulated work of art, with its controlled and interlocking system of significant devices—has given way before what can only be called a declaration of independence. It is, among other things, a Reader's Rights Movement which has restored to the reader as obedient subject an exhilarating freedom of movement.

What got discombobulated? The autotelic work of literature, its pristine immanence carefully surrounded by the heresies and the fallacies (affective, intentional, paraphrastic) which guarded the portals of its splen-

From New Literary History, Volume XIII, Spring 1982. Copyright © 1982 by New Literary History. The University of Virginia.

did isolation. Once it gave good value, that doctrine, that methodology. To one who, like myself, of all moving things in literature finds intelligible form the most moving, it supplied a working lifetime of beauties and insights. But since self-consuming artifacts, strange loops, infinite regresses, gaps, voids, and anxieties of influence have come into our lives, the critic's occupation has become at once more hazardous and more inspiriting than when we were the officially delegated tourist guides to a carefully fenced-off nature reserve of canonical and exemplary works.

One of those canonical and exemplary works has been, for sixty years now, *The Waste Land*. It presents us with, appropriately enough in a field thick with them, our first paradox, or strange loop, in time. T.S. Eliot, one of the fathers of the New Critical sensibility, with its bias toward the objective, the unsentimental, the dispassionate, the rational, the technical, knitted into or mapped somehow onto a Romantic, organicist, intuitionist aesthetic—a knitting and a mapping which were to flutter the critical dovecotes for three generations—T.S. Eliot was also the founding father of New Criticism's devourer. We are told that such family cannibalism is literary criticism in a nutshell. Be that as it may, it is my thesis at present that *The Waste Land*, that seminal modernist poem of 1922, can now be read as a postmodernist poem of 1982: as a deconstructionist Ur-text, even as a Deconstructionist Manifesto. It was paradoxical enough then that radical modernism found its spokesman in the most conservative of converts to a most conservative and hierarchical church. History has its revenges, and if we speak of the irony of family romance, it is worth noticing that the chief deconstructionist critics ignore T.S. Eliot with a pointed contempt which amounts to a concerted effort to discanonize him. Just as, indeed, of all the authors quoted or alluded to in *The Waste Land*, Wordsworth, Shelley, and Tennyson, his own true precursors, do not (overtly) appear at all.

The Waste Land exploded upon the world with an effect of total incomprehension. Yeats said it gave the impression of a man "helpless before the contents of his own mind." Leavis said, "It would be difficult to imagine a more complete projection of awareness, but . . . there are ways in which it is possible to be too conscious—and conscious of too much—that is the plight."

In the heyday of New Criticism it was customary to attempt to unify *The Waste Land*. Cleanth Brooks himself took the lead with one of the most distinguished and valuable essays of this kind. "Most of its critics," he says, "misconceive entirely the theme and the structure of the poem. There has been little or no attempt to deal with it as a unified whole." He thereupon marshals the whole battery of New Critical exegesis to show that the thematic "contrast between two kinds of life and two kinds of death," the parallel symbolism of fertility cults and resurrection, and the juxtapositional structure which ironically reveals the dissimilarity in surface similarities and the fundamental similarity in apparent dissimilarities all work toward the buttressing of a masked and indirect but unequivocal statement of Christian belief.

It is my objective in this paper to show that, on the contrary, disunification, or desedimentation, or dissemination (to use Derridean terminology) is the *raison d'être* of the poem; that in it the strategies of self-consumption, *mise en abyme*, and influence anxiety can be inspected at large; and that if one wanted a concise account of it, one could not do better than to quote Derrida himself on his own practice: it exhibits throughout "a certain strategic arrangement, which, within the field and its own powers, turn[s] against itself its own stratagems, produc[ing] a force of dislocation which spreads itself through the whole system, splitting it in all directions and delimiting it through and through."

Let us begin with deconstructive strategies of the simpler kind: in *The Waste Land* the fundamental categories of literary discourse are dismantled or simply abandoned. There is no narrative, there is no time, though there are "withered stumps of time," and no place—or rather there is no single time or place but a constant, bewildering shifting and disarray of times and places; there is no unifying central character either speaking or spoken about, no protagonist or antagonist, no drama, no epic, no lyric, though there are moments suggestive of all these generic constellations. As is well known, Eliot's note announces that Tiresias, "although a mere spectator and not indeed a 'character', is yet the most important personage in the poem, uniting all the rest. What Tiresias *sees*, in fact, is the substance of the poem." But just as all the women melt into each other, and all the sailors and merchants, so Tiresias, the prophet of Thebes, melts into a number of prophetic or quasi-prophetic figures: the Cumean sibyl, Ezekiel, Isaiah, Madame Sosostris. And if what Tiresias sees is the substance of the poem, there is no reason why the substance is not also what the Cumean sibyl sees as she contemplates those grains of sand in her hand, which include Tiresias and Ezekiel and Isaiah (or vice versa) and Madame Sosostris, and hence what she sees in her tarot pack, or what Eliot sees, who, conventionally received, is the overseer of all these seers.

Beyond this *mise en abyme* of seers, or ventriloquism of voices, there is no one point of view, no single style, idiom, register, or recurrent and therefore linking linguistic device which could define a subject, in the sense of a dominant speaking or projecting persona. The "poet's mind" for which we are accustomed to seek is indeterminately catalyzer and/or catalyzed. Nor, similarly, can we differentiate a subject in the sense of an overall subject matter, or argument, or myth, or theme for the poem to be unequivocally about or to embody. I say nothing of the absence of obvious conventional poetic features such as meter, rhyme, stanza, or any regularity or recurrence or set of symmetries which could constitute formal pattern in any classical sense at all. It is totally, radically nonintegrative and antidiscursive, its parts connected by neither causes, effects, parallelism, nor antithesis. It is a cinematographic mélange or montage of glimpses, gestures, images, echoes, voices, phrases, memories, fragments of speech, song, quotation, appearances, and disappearances. It consists of a plethora of signifiers in complete discomplementarity with any set or sequence of recognizably related signifieds in a represented world. It is an apogee of fragmentation and discontinuity, referring, if at all, only to itself. But this self that it is constituted by what it is not, its presence is made up of its absences, its gaps and ellipses are the fountainheads of its significance, its disorder its order. If we compare it to the other early stream-of-consciousness poems—*Prufrock, Portrait of a Lady, Rhapsody on a Windy Night*, even *Preludes* and *Gerontion*—we see at once the radicalization of the irrational and the incoherent which has taken place. There there are personae and stories to be descried. There are figure and ground. Here none.

Nor do its symbols function as foci. They refuse to symbolize. They explode and proliferate. They turn themselves inside out, diffuse their meanings, and collapse back again into disarticulated images. Those are pearls that were his eyes, but is this a life image or a death image? Is water, or the sea, death or life? Is fire a lust of the flesh or the purity of the spirit? City, Garden, Desert, River—the great symbolic topoi—are all Janus-faced, multivalent, ambiguous. City, the "city," the unreal city, Jerusalem, Athens, Alexandria, Vienna, London, "cracks and reforms and bursts in the violet air." The Hyacinth garden is Adonis's garden, is the sylvan scene, is "the heart of light, the silence." In the desert of broken images, stony rubbish, "dead mountain mouth of carious teeth that cannot spit," there is shadow under the red rock, your shadow in the morning, your shadow at evening. The Thames, the Ganges, the Rhine, the Euphrates—are they one river or many? Thick with accretions and supplements, are they opaque with the opacity of the concrete, or transparent lamps around a spiritual flame, unified, abstract, conceptual? Or are these possibilities in unceasing dialectical interchange: idea and image, essence and existence, appearance and reality? And if, wise after the Freudian event, we say, Ah, but there is a language which this mode of symbolic phantasmagoria resembles, the language of the unconscious, with its condensations, substitutions, displacements, and are then challenged to find an interpretative key to this dream, we cannot.

Like dreams this text has no beginning or end. It could begin anywhere and end anywhere because it has no inception and no center and no closure. If "Shantih Shantih Shantih" sounds like an end, both in the sense of telos and of cessation, it also and at the same time is only one fragment in the plethora of dissociated fragments—"These fragments I have shored against my ruins"—with which the last section terminates, its first person indissolubly interentangling past and present, outside and inside. Extra- or intertextually, this section alludes to the Fisher King, Isaiah, an English nursery rhyme, the story of Arnaut Daniel in *The Purgatorio*, *The Pervigilium Veneris* or Ovid's *Metamorphoses*, de Nerval's "The Disinherited," *The Spanish Tragedy*, *The Upanishads*. Intratextually it picks up the themes of fertility/infertility, prophecy, apocalypse, sexuality and homosexuality, spring renewal and its inversion, violation and flight, life-in-death and death-in-life, loss, grief, passion and madness, plays within plays, appearance and reality, and redemption or nonredemption. But which? Does "Shantih Shantih Shantih" bring us, ironically, back to base, to the forgetful snow of "The Burial of the Dead," irremediably unredeemed, or does it not? Does it open to a transcendent world and close a fallen one, a prison in which each, thinking of the key, confirms the prison? Shall these bones live? Or shall they be only picked in whispers by the sea? or rattled by the rat's foot? Shall these bones live, does the poem say, or shall only the corpse in the garden sprout and bloom?

Have we a poem at all? An Antipoem? It oversteps its own frame: Baudelaire's "You! hypocrite lecture!—mon semblable,—mon frere," like the hand seeming to come right out of the enlistment poster of 1916, transforms author into audience or vice versa, or both into each other's double. But is there an author at all? *Il miglior fabbro*, when you look through the *Facsimile*, was, it seems, not only the better craftsman but the only craftsman. Is what Ezra Pound omitted part of the poem or not? Part of the "original" poem? Or is the original poem now Pound's? What is "original"? Tradition, speaking in the actual phrases of countless dead European authors, or the individual talent's, Eliot's or Pound's? Author, referent, reader, language, message (to read round Jakobson's model of functions) have all been dislocated or deconstructed and the result is to foil and confound every attempt to construe a total meaning or to provide a unified or single interpretation out of whole cloth.

Have we a whole at all? The poem is divided into parts which are subdivided into parts, for which no rationale of part and whole is evident. One could reallocate the parts at any point with no noticeable consequence to the overall effect, and with no noticeable effect upon the innumerable exegeses which have been attempted. There is, and there is not, a seasonal order suggested. It is adumbrated only to be evaded. The poem begins with spring—a cruelly deconstructed spring to be sure, but undeniably April. In Part III, "The Fire Sermon," "The river's tent is broken: the last fingers of leaf / Clutch and sink into the wet bank." It is autumn. But there is no hint of a season in II and IV, unless we press for it: the ladies in "A Game of Chess" are perhaps, however frustratedly or dispiritedly, in the summer of their lives, and death, by water or otherwise, is homologous with winter. That gives us a deconstructed seasonal cycle, consummated or abrogated by the apocalyptic, trans-temporal fifth part with its thunder speaking out of the whirlwind. But this does not help us to find out what the poem, as opposed to the thunder, says. One could pick up a hint of structure from the quinquepartite division and attempt to construct a five-act dramatic order. A five-act antidrama, of course, since there is no protagonist, no dramatic action, and no outcome. But we can read a predicament of sorts into Part I: loss of faith and hope and vitality, and a follow-through in II with its unhappy and crisscrossed human relations (even a Shakespearean double plot, if you will, with high life and low life counterpointed and contrasted). Part III offers a large number of crises and reversals in love: betrayals, adulteries, seductions, errors, and mistaken identities (Tiresias is confused even about his own). Phlebas suggests a point of nihilistic despair, or possibly the hint of a countermovement toward transcendent remedy, and "What the Thunder Said" is catastrophe as apocalypse. But even as deconstructed drama, *The Waste Land* offers us no way to determine whether the thrust of its nonoutcome is tragic or comic. Its fifth-act recognition may be either a tragic recollapsing into temporal ruin and chaos or a divinely comic resolution of all previous perplexities through the magic formula: give, sympathize, control, and the peace that passeth understanding.

The radical indeterminacy of *The Waste Land* has provoked a number of recuperative strategies. T.S. Eliot himself was characteristically noncommittal. It was a rhythmical grumble, he said. But he also pointed weightily in the direction of reconstructed myth: *The Golden Bough* with its slain and risen gods, Jessie Weston's pursuit of the Grail legend in *From Ritual to Romance*, with its barren Fisher King and its Questing Knight. Moving on from these clues, it has been possible to read *The Waste Land* as a sermon in disguise (as did Cleanth Brooks), preaching a Christian message in Brahman disguise. A countermove was the attempt to read it as no more than a gift for his Imagist friend, the as yet unachieved long poem in the Imagist mode: a mosaic of objective correlatives or images—intellectual and emotional "complexes" in instants of time—with none of the stigmata of the discursive, abstract, or sentimental against which Pound inveighed in his Credo. Internalized versions of these readings make it a latent conversion poem in which the preconversion experience of sex disgust, self-disgust, alienation, sterility, and failure hovers, so to speak, on the brink of transformation or transcendence (Eliot's actual conversion took place, it will be remembered, in 1927), and the poem can be seen retrospectively in that event's long shadow; or it is simply the inscribing of a nightmare, a literal dream, death-obsessed, saturated with death imagery in both of its climates—snow death and desert death—and with the grotesque fantasyings and defenses of primary fear. Just as all of Eliot's poetry can be seen as a self-consuming dialectic in which flight from subjectivity (or "personality") becomes a flight into extreme subjectivity, so *The Waste Land* has been read in similarly polarized ways: as an objectivist panorama of the decadent times, with the Fisher King as tutelary protagonist and Spengler of *The Decline of the West* as tutelary genius; and on the other hand as a deeply personal elegy, like its precursors, *Lycidas*, *Adonais*, and *In Memoriam*, mourning a friend lost at sea but, unlike them, dismantling itself as elegy and dissimulating its intimate motivations, expressing and not expressing them, on account of the unresolved guilt and anxiety the poet's relations with Jean Verdenal, "mort aux Dardanelles," evidently entailed.

An irreducible plurality of meaning, of course, is no news to literary critics, and would not in itself justify the title of this paper. If, however, deconstruction has been no more than the valorizing of plurality to a point where no vestige of embarrassment stemming from the rationalist, universalist traditions of thought is left, even that would bring *The Waste Land*, with its extremist aesthetic of irrationality and the infinite regress of its discontinuities, firmly into the orbit. But I believe there is more to it than this. T.S. Eliot's own "mythical method," which he attributed to Joyce and Yeats as initiators—the manipulation of a continuous parallel between contemporaneity and antiquity, which made, he said, the modern world possible in art—is identical twin to Harari's account of Derrida's deconstruction: "The tracing of a path among textual strata in order to stir up and expose forgotten and dormant sediments of meaning." And if, according to Derrida, "a text is a text only if it conceals, from the first glance, from the first comer, the law of its composition and the rules of its game," then Eliot's text positively out-Herods Herod. And to make this clear I would like to add a deconstructive footnote to Eliot's famous footnotes.

As everyone knows, something was required to fill out the printer's extra pages. What more suitable padding for a Harvard philosophy graduate than a little academic apparatus? Twenty-four years later he himself joked about "bogus scholarship." But is that what it is? First of all, it is a parody of academic footnoting. Everything bibliographical recorded in it is undoubtedly true. One can check. But it is so far from being exhaustive or comprehensive that it is, by default, more misleading than leading. Quite a few of the notes record a chance association in the author's memory (for which, of course, we have only his word), as if he were helpfully providing a future Livingston Lowes with material for a *Road to Timbuctoo*. And the combination of these two modes, the quasi-encyclopedic and the quasi-introspective, puts deconstructively into question the whole matter of sources, origins, traces, parasites and hosts, and the civil liberties of readers.

Middleton's *Women beware Women* is quoted for "A Game of Chess" but not, significantly, the more obviously evoked game of chess between Ferdinand and Miranda in *The Tempest*, which is massively present through Ariel's ditty, "this music crept by me upon the waters," and "the king my brother's wreck." Hallucinations occurring on Antarctic expeditions will surely be less resonant to most readers than the unseen presence of Christ on the road to Emmaus. Most deadpan of all perhaps is the laconic "A phenomenon which I have often noticed" for "With a dead sound on the final stroke of nine"—the hour, according to Christian hagiography, of the crucifixion; or the treating of a London County Council pamphlet, "The Proposed Demolition of Nineteen City Churches," as equivalent in status to a work by Dante, Virgil, or Milton. Is he not throwing into deliberate disarray all the paraphernalia which represent the rational order and hierarchy and mastery of knowledge, of the mind? We are informed of the obviously nonaccidental collocation of Buddha and St. Augustine as the "representatives of eastern and western asceticism," and we have F.H. Bradley brought to gloss a line which is as lucid as the sun, while the truly opaque and mysterious connections and disconnections of the poem are left in fathomless obscurity. Yet at the same time the Notes chart a number of tracings (significant? insignificant?) through the epochs of his imagination, which are, however, no more and no less authoritative than the language of the poem itself. And the question remains open: Are the Notes a part or not a part of *The Waste Land*? If they are supplementary, what do they supplement? The poem on the page? The poem in the author's or implied author's mind? The poem in any reader's mind? The poem which itself has become a supplement to the whole corpus of European literature that it quotes, and within the drama of which it acts its play? These supplements themselves, as they add, so they displace or replace, just as the Hermit thrush's song of the Notes, unequalled for "purity and sweetness of tone and exquisite modulation," supplements and displaces/replaces the unheard song of the absent bird of the poem, present only by proxy in the imagined sound of the water drops: Drip drop drip drop drop drop drop.

Thus the final deconstructive act of *The Waste Land* deconstructs distinctions between critic and author, "fiction" and "fact," presentation and representation, origin and supplement. These are the classic, central deconstructionist themes. Deconstructionists will know better than I what profit they may derive from this Ur-text of their creed. But at least we may all feel freed at last in our readings of a superimposed message, an indoctrination, an obligation to the definitive.

"Perhaps," said Yeats, to conclude once again with the words of Eliot's great rival and antagonist, "Perhaps in this new, profound poetry, the symbol itself is contradictory, horror of life, horror of death."

GREGORY S. JAY

Ghosts and Roses

Follow the feet
Of the walker, the water-thrush. Follow the flight
Of the dawning arrow, the purple martin. Greet
In silence the bullbat. All are delectable. Sweet sweet sweet
But resign this land at the end, resign it
To its true owner, the tough one, the sea-gull.
The palaver is finished.

from "Cape Ann"

In part 5 of "The Dry Salvages" the seas and sailors drop away. The poet begins his turn toward exploration of another approach to ecstasy, one that will culminate in the "double part" he assumes when he meets the ghost in "Little Gidding." As "The Dry Salvages" closes, the chaos of interpretative methods ("these are usual / Pastimes and drugs") motivates the recurrent hope of order: "But to apprehend / The point of intersection of the timeless / With time, is an occupation for the saint." Thus, "For most of us, there is only the unattended / Moment, the moment in and out of time," the again repeated moment "lost in a shaft of sunlight, / The wild thyme unseen, or the winter lightning." These new repetitions are now "hints and guesses" pointing to the Christian philosophy of a divine repetition: "The hint half-guessed, the gift half understood, is Incarnation." The Incarnation is God's strange repetition in time, as Christ figures the archetype of the revisionist. He is the ideal *figura* of which personal repetitions are prefigurations, as they seek the Spirit of the moment in representative reembodiments.

From *T.S. Eliot and the Poetics of Literary History*. Copyright © 1983 by Louisiana State University Press.

One poetic "saint" who glimpsed this mystery is Dante, whose *Paradiso* concludes with puzzlement at "our image" in the divine Light and with a reconciliation among the stars: "I wished to see how the image conformed to the circle and how it has its place therein; but my own wings were not sufficient for that, save that my mind was smitten by a flash wherein its wish came to it. Here power failed the lofty phantasy; but already my desire and my will were revolved, like a wheel that is evenly moved, by the Love which moves the sun and the other stars" (*Paradiso*, canto 33). By a fiery flash of the divine, Dante receives the mystery, but cannot record it, for his receptive faculty for images ("fantasia") remains human. He experiences an Annunciation of the Word made flesh; yet, its representation is reserved for the Word itself, while the poet's words record the feeling of this illumination. Love is the emotion of divinity, the unrepresentable height and depth inspiring poet and universe. Dante carries away a souvenir of this passionate moment in his poetic remembrance; his vision is not of the mystery's solution, but of the revolving love of its repetition in time. Eliot alludes to this moment in Dante ("to my thinking the highest point that poetry has ever reached or ever can reach") to prepare the way for his own version of the *Paradiso* in "Little Gidding." His love for Dante's poem moves him to attempt its reincarnation. He will end his own climactic work by repeating the end of Dante's, and the approach to its meaning will in this other time alter Dante in yet another fulfillment of the mystery's promise.

Fire is the element of "Little Gidding." The refining purgatorial fire now burns with enlightenment, as the pentecostal flame and the flash of Dante. As "un fulgore" had shown the Incarnation to Dante, so Dante will be reincarnated and show himself in Eliot's poem. This meeting of the living and the dead crosses the normal categories of time and bestows meaning upon them through other patterns. "Little Gidding" transfigures the occupation of the saint, finds in its intertextuality the "intersection of the timeless / With time." This violation of temporal rules recalls the simultaneous order of literature in "Tradition and the Individual Talent" and gives a dramatic account of such an encounter between the disciple and "some dead master." Thus, when the scene is set, it is "Midwinter spring," a confusion of the regulated order imposed on phenomena and called "natural." Designations of identity are exposed as reductions of the mystery. This undoing of classifications parallels the earlier sense that "Words strain, / Crack and sometimes break, under the burden" of stamping a single identity on disparate objects by obscuring the difference that makes possible the abstraction producing the signifier. Those trained in the ways of comparative philology, such as Nietzsche and Eliot, were quick to probe the philological relativity of language. Eliot assimilated this questioning of the signifier to his own systematic interrogation of language and emotion, locating the problem in the process of representation, or what he called remembrance: "In perception we intend the object; in recollection we intend a complex which is composed of image and feeling. We do not intend to remember simply the object, but the object as we remember it. And this new object is much more *the experience* than the *past object*, for we try to remember how we felt toward the past object" (KE, 49). A word repeats conventionally, limiting meaning. Poetic repetition "unknowns" words and moments in another discourse. They pass through exile into humiliation, their repetition signaling love and their remembrance incarnating the spirit that knows, or unknows, itself through them.

This interpretative process is "Suspended in time, between pole and tropic," antinomies undone by the "pentecostal fire" that "Stirs the dumb spirit" to transfigured speech of "the spring time . . . not in time's convenant. . . . Not in the scheme of generation." The exploration leads not to the eternal, for that would be only the timeless, but to the "uncertain hour before the morning" in section 2, when the "unimaginable" trods the pavement. We have come ashore, as at the end of *The Waste Land*, but these lands are in a very strange order. Their principle of conjunction is not unlike that binding the fragments and quotes at the end of the earlier poem. What is different is the absence of hysteria, the calm passion of this entrance into that that passeth understanding. The "broken king" comes again, dethroned, repeating the Fisher King and King Charles, now humbled, without hope or fear of restoration to authority. Here "at the end of the journey" knight and poet discover the errancy that disrupts the "scheme of generation," turning each word and each accomplishment into prelude and benediction.

> And what you thought you came for
> Is only a shell, a husk of meaning
> From which the purpose breaks only when it is fulfilled
> If at all. Either you had no purpose
> Or the purpose is beyond the end you figured
> And is altered in fulfilment.
>
> (LG, I)

Undoing the temporal and historical structure of figural interpretation, Eliot's fulfillments break their *figurae*, reach back and alter the purposes of signs.

The fulfillment here is not the original figure in a different, exalted form that had been prefigured: rather these fulfillments choose their past figures, empty them, and make them "only a shell, a husk of meaning." Figural interpretation had resolved the ambiguity of original and copy inherent in the etymology of *figura* by the construction of a teleological model of figural purposes. The times were reconciled by the links to the logos figural interpretation assumed; the new testaments emptied the authority of the old

and inverted their priority, turning them into hints and guesses of themselves, the new texts. Although the doctrine described a movement forward
from figure to fulfillment, the actual motion ran backward as the modern
moment secured itself by revising the purposeful significance of the ancient.
The poet, then, working at this actual level, accepts the inevitable transfiguration of his authority and words by others in their interpretations, accepts
the new worlds of meaning that break, "If at all," beyond the end the poet
figured, constantly altering his text in new fulfillments. It would be hard to
believe that Eliot was unaware of the theory of the figural and of the history of
the term, especially in light of his modest education in Romance philology
and his assimilation of the Christian historiographical model. In any case, the
essence of the practice is contained in Augustine's *Confessions* and in Dante's
Commedia, two of Eliot's principal inspirations. Eliot's transfigurational poetics emerge as a revision of Christian historiography and theology, English
political history, the literature of remembrance and autobiography, the philosophy of belated perception, the literary criticism of historical formalism, and
his own personal quest for a reconciliation with America and mutability.

Figural breaks are the eternal recurrence of "the world's end" repeating "in place and time, / Now and in England." A simple notion of the end of
history would still involve "mere sequence— / Or even development."
"Little Gidding" puts an end to the end of history and begins history as altered
repetitions, a constant intersection.

> And what the dead had no speech for, when living,
> They can tell you, being dead: the communication
> Of the dead is tongued with fire beyond the language of the living.
>
> (LG, 1)

Thus, the theoretical model is propounded and ready for application in the
conjuration of a dead master speaking in fiery tongues.

> In the uncertain hour before the morning
>   Near the ending of interminable night
>   At the recurrent end of the unending
> After the dark dove with the flickering tongue
>   Had passed below the horizon of his homing
>   While the dead leaves still rattled on like tin
> Over the asphalt where no other sound was
>   Between three districts whence the smoke arose
>   I met one walking, loitering and hurried
> As if blown towards me like the metal leaves
>   Before the urban dawn wind unresisting.
>   And as I fixed upon the down-turned face
> That pointed scrutiny with which we challenge
>   The first-met stranger in the waning dusk
>   I caught the sudden look of some dead master

Whom I had known, forgotten, half recalled
  Both one and many; in the brown baked features
  The eyes of a familiar compound ghost
Both intimate and unidentifiable.
  So I assumed a double part, and cried
  And heard another's voice cry: "What! are *you* here?"
                                                    (LG, II)

Forgotten and half-recalled, intimate and unidentifiable, the familiar compound ghost characterizes the eerie temporality and mixed identities of the literary text. This meeting and conversation may be read as Eliot's condensed summary of his poetic philosophy, the last act and statement of the individual's struggle with inheritance and futurity. In "What Dante Means to Me" (1950), Eliot says, "This section of a poem—not the length of one canto of the Divine Comedy—cost me far more time and trouble than any passage of the same length that I have ever written" (CC, 129). The recently published manuscripts of the poem prove the point.

The conception was clear at the start: an "imitation" of Dante's terza rima, a reenactment of the master-disciple scenes Eliot so often cited, the compounding of Yeats with Dante, Shelley, and others, and the echo of Hamlet's ghost. But in the first draft the concluding advice given by this ghost, some twenty-four lines, treats other themes than the published text. The distance between the warden and the ghost appears greater, the alienation more severe. "I was always dead," the speaker says in one version of their meeting, "Always revived, and always something other, / And he a face changing." Recalling King Hamlet's "Remember me," the manuscript ghost's answering injunction is of a different sort.

Remember rather the essential moments
  That were the times of birth and death and change
  The agony and the solitary vigil.
Remember also fear, loathing and hate,
  The wild strawberries eaten in the garden,
  The walls of Poitiers, and the Anjou wine,
The fresh new season's rope, the smell of varnish
  On the clean oar, the drying of the sails,
Such things as seem of least and most importance.
So, as you circumscribe this dreary round,
  Shall your life pass from you, with all you hated
  And all you loved, the future and the past.
United to another past, another future,
  (After many seas and after many lands)
  The dead and the unborn, who shall be nearer
Than the voices and the faces that were most near.

The *Quartets* sometimes fall to flatness of cadence and sense in the pursuit of a common style. The recourse to Eliot's cherished nautical imagery suggests the importance of this section, but it comes out a pale reflection of "The Dry Salvages." This version lapses into vagueness compared to the final copy, its reconciliation seemingly unearned and complacent. Its defect, as Eliot wrote in a letter to John Hayward, was "the lack of some acute personal reminiscence."

He supplies the personal touch through Yeats's influence, inspired by the late lyrics of tragic gay wisdom. Not surprisingly, the 1940 essay on Yeats focuses on influence and maturity. While writing the *Quartets*, Eliot sets down in his appreciation of Yeats the poetic principle guiding his own work, finally admitting the primacy of a "second impersonality" wherein the poet makes a general symbol of his personal experience (OPP, 299). Redefining himself through Yeats, Eliot offers in this essay his mature position on language and social change. It is important for an understanding of the *Quartets'* approach to the meaning of current, catastrophic historical experiences. Embodied in the *Quartets*, and in numerous essays of the period after 1939, this attitude culminated a debate that had begun in *The Sacred Wood's* attack on Arnold: "Born into a world in which the doctrine of 'Art for Art's sake' was generally accepted, and living on into one in which art has been asked to be instrumental to social purposes, he held firmly to the right view which is between these, though not in any way a compromise between them, and showed that an artist, by serving his art with entire integrity, is at the same time rendering the greatest service he can to his own nation and to the whole world" (OPP, 307).

For all Yeats's importance, however, Dante still dominates the compound. Of him, Eliot says "that of the very few poets of similar stature there is none, not even Virgil, who has been a more attentive student of the *art* of poetry, or a more scrupulous, painstaking and *conscious* practitioner of the *craft*" (CC, 132). Having already written extensively on Dante, Eliot in 1950 means "to talk informally about his influence upon myself," in particular about the philosophy behind the composition of "Little Gidding." He does so in a technical manner, like Poe's account of how he wrote "The Raven," an account the veracity of which Eliot himself doubted (CC, 29-35). So we may also suspect Eliot's retrospect. The concentration on craft turns the passage's "rending pain of re-enactment" into only a craftsman's training. This half-truth eludes admission of the pain of comparing one's own soul to those of the Yeatses and the Dantes.

Eliot spends the first pages of his last Dante essay on the theory of poetic debts, citing his own enrichment by Laforgue and Baudelaire. He reiterates his belief that the young poet should apprentice himself to minor poets, but with his usual genealogical metaphors he cautions that the older poet can learn little unless he faces "exalted . . . distant ancestors" and "great masters," as Dante faced Virgil and as Eliot tried to face Yeats and Dante and Shakespeare. Confessing his earlier anxiety of influence, Eliot now sees how the mature poet can only rise by competition with the great, who will not leave him alone anyway. Praising Shelley's "translation" of Dante in "The Triumph of Life" as better than his own, he states that "the influence of Dante, where it is really powerful, is a *cumulative* influence: that is, the older you grow, the stronger the domination becomes" (CC, 130). "Little Gidding" submits to this domination while inscribing it in the same structure of revisionary control over the precursors pioneered by Dante. This repetition lessens the threat, paying back old debts and stamping new coinages as palimpsests on the old.

Eliot has "ranged over some varieties of 'influence' in order to approach an indication, by contrast, of what Dante has meant to me" (CC, 128). In *The Waste Land*, he recounts, he intended to "establish a relationship between the medieval inferno and modern life," insinuating that to forget Dante, or any past's potential, is a sin of the modern inferno, a symptom if not a cause of its pernicious ennui. The parallel works in "Little Gidding," too, written in reaction to the repetition that was World War II: "But the method is different: here I was debarred from quoting or adapting at length—I borrowed and adapted freely only a few phrases—because I was imitating" (CC, 128). Imitation here acts like translation and transfiguration, differentiated from the shoring of archaeologized ruins. The recollection of pieces joins a larger metamorphic repetition of style, stance, and theme as Eliot identifies with the dead master. If the transumption prevails and the dead join in chorus with the living, then the poetic father does become "like an admired elder brother." In the scheme of generations the anxiety of domination forms a hierarchy of fathers and sons, disparate rival temporalities. In the scheme of poetry, "not in time's covenant," matured poets are as brothers, contemporaneous and adjacent colleagues. Imitation disciplines the poem with a high linguistic standard. The poem undergoes askesis, metering the transfusion from other authors. As Eliot said of Yeats, "The course of improvement is towards a greater and greater starkness" (OPP, 305). The same is said of Dante (CC, 129).

The common stylistic effort, tied to a theme of the "gifts reserved for age," replaces the quest for individual authority, except as it can be made to symbolize the general. Through imitation or repetition, originality exists as the compound of what Dantesque standards can produce through the contemporary poet. In this case, repetition is not death, not the sign of exhausted sensibility or the horror of meaningless recurrence. It is the shared project of poets. Repetition and imitation order history. They interpret discontinuity by an abstraction of the Same, yet remain open to the altered fulfillments wrought by desire, accident, and fate. Thus, Eliot brings Dante to bear upon the morning after an air raid, a modern moment of breakage brought to comprehension by imitation, and the resulting poem supplements what was once the meaning of the *Commedia*. Eliot's emphasis on technique implies that one sustenance he seeks in that morning is the renewed assurance that the tongues of poetic fire can match those of material destruction. The submission of the poem to an impersonal linguistic goal coincides with the effort to place an eruptive event in a consoling frame.

Seven of the first eight lines of the imitation begin with prepositional or adverbial phrases. The syntax dramatizes the key act of placement, difficult when time and seasons are suspended. As Hugh Kenner has noted, "no other *Quartet* is so explicitly located in time as this one in which time is conquered." Still, the reiteration of "In . . . Near . . . At . . . After . . . While . . . Over . . . Between" speaks of a profound difficulty of location. The reader and the text meet, as do the warden and the ghost, at an uncertain intersection of poetic crossroads, turning the streets of London into a literary labyrinth. Eliot's lines are in the first person, but deceptively so, for the singular identity of this "I" is immediately denied by the reader's knowledge that his is the Dantesque "I" as well. This "I" is neither Eliot nor Dante nor any other poet, but an intertextual compound ("I was always dead, / Always revived, and always something other"), "the recognition of a temperament akin to one's own, and in another aspect the discovery of one's own form. These are not two things, but two aspects of the same thing" (CC, 126). And the encounter cannot be wholly located in the text, for it is with "That pointed scrutiny with which we challenge / The first-met stranger in the waning dusk" that "I caught the sudden look of some dead master." The insertion of the universalizing "we" depersonalizes the encounter, reminding us as readers that the scene is also an allegory of our own meeting with this text, that we are also the "I" and Eliot is also "some dead master." This prefiguration recalls the mix of "I" and "you" in "Song of Myself," which enables a metamorphosis of author into text, text into the fulfilled meaning of the text, meaning into the identity of the reader. Whitman's final lines are also outside time's covenant, in literature's simultaneity. Self-consciously, Whitman's poem addresses the reader across the decades, marking the text as crossroads.

> You will hardly know who I am or what I mean
> But I shall be good health to you nevertheless
> And filter and fibre your blood.
>
> Failing to fetch me at first keep encouraged,
> Missing me one place search another,
> I stop somewhere waiting for you.

We should also recall the time-traveling of "Crossing Brooklyn Ferry." The uncanny Whitman enters the compound, master of temporal shuttlings and shuffler of pronominal identities.

The "double part" Eliot plays does the poets in different voices. Ecstatic, he is beside himself and compounded, "still the same, / Knowing myself yet being someone other." He is "being" in the "other" as the "other" lives through him, "In concord at this intersection time / Of meeting nowhere." He speaks to himself. The dialogue that follows is the self-reflection of the present conducted through the past, reflected across time and meant to prepare the future. So compounded beyond time, this ghost, unlike Hamlet's father, does not command the son to a stultifying obedience.

> Last season's fruit is eaten
> And the fullfed beast shall kick the empty pail.
> For last year's words belong to last year's language
> And next year's words await another voice.

The ghost tacitly approves Eliot's method, rehearsing its thought and theory while forgiving them. As he is soon to acknowledge, this theory makes his own existence possible in the untimely dawn of this text. The ghost consecrates the poem's askesis, its clear-sighted submission to the ravages of time. The "fullfed beast" aptly images the cycle of poetic usurpation that Bloom has schematized and that Eliot accepts as fate. The distance between timebound languages, here seemingly so irrevocable, closes even as it is pronounced: this is an imitation of Dante and Yeats, and it does manage to bring "last year's words" to life again in "another voice." Kenner says that "no other Voice in Eliot's repertoire articulates with such authority."

But what is the nature of this authority, and by whom has it been authored? Eliot constructs his authority by a mingled borrowing of tomes and tones. We feel the ghost's authority because a poet has craftily shaped him that way: the ghost is an allegory of authority, built consciously out of the rhetoric of wisdom. This authority is a ghost, the nonpresence and nonabsence of sunlit truth, a compound whose persuasive voice depends on convention, history, and humility. Eliot had once found Yeats "perhaps a little too much the weather-worn Triton among the streams," quoting "Vacillation," a poem consciously appropriated by "Little Gidding" (ASG, 45-46). Eliot works to save his poem from the charge by taming Yeats with Dante. Eliot steals their authority and then makes it speak in his own measure, in the passage where Yeats' dancer moves in Dante's "refining fire."

The fate of ghostly authority sung, "the passage now presents no hindrance / To the spirit unappeased and peregrine / Between two worlds become much like each other." Translated from the distant shore of Hades, the ghost depends on the present and the poet for life and authority, and vice versa. Ritually murdered by beasts, his resurrection can be of use to "next year's words." Feeling the need to mute the voice of Yeats, Eliot inserts a translation of Mallarmé: "Since our concern was speech, and speech impelled us to purify the dialect of the tribe." The allusion, from "The Tomb of Edgar Poe," compounds Mallarmé, Eliot, and Poe together in the craftsman's task. Mallarmé's poem, however, bitterly protests the hostility and incomprehension that met Poe's work.

> Just as eternity transforms him at last unto Himself,
> The Poet rouses with a naked sword
> His age terrified at not having discerned
> That death was triumphant in that strange voice.

It required French translation and imitation to resurrect Poe or at least to mark his grave (a story of transatlantic influence Eliot tells in "From Poe to Valéry" [CC, 27-42]). The dismal ignominy suffered by Poe and revenged by Mallarmé inspires Eliot's own funereal colloquy, his tomb of Dante, Yeats, Poe, Shelley, Mallarmé, Shakespeare, Whitman, Swift and others. Eliot cannot assume Mallarmé's resentful tone, because he is himself a part of the compound. Yeats's voice returns to deliver the final advice on the ironic, sad "gifts reserved for age / To set a crown upon your lifetime's effort," as Mallarmé's crown for Poe becomes Eliot's Yeatsian crown of thorns.

The embarrassment Eliot feels at the Triton's weathered reflections on his aged self prompts him to divide his echo, severing the counsel of wisdom from introspection by dramatically representing it as speech to a disciple. Though the words pertain to the ghost's experience, the pronouns and tone are carefully restricted to avoid self-pity and direct attention toward the aspirant. We sense that these sufferings have been the ghost's, but his particular experience is no more than the general symbol. "First, the cold friction of expiring sense" robs the sensual and sexual of power "As body and soul begin to fall asunder." To this loss of physical powers is added "the conscious impotence of rage / At human folly, and the laceration / Of laughter at what ceases to amuse." These might be the Sweeney poems or the vitriol of *After Strange Gods*.

Such attitudes, self-centered and superior, must yield to the wisdom of humility and repetition.

> And last, the rending pain of re-enactment
> Of all that you have done, and been; the shame
> Of motives late revealed, and the awareness
> Of things ill done and done to others' harm
> Which you took for exercise of virtue.
> Then fools' approval stings, and honour stains.
> From wrong to wrong the exasperated spirit

Proceeds, unless restored by that refining fire
Where you must move in measure, like a dancer.

The rending pain of reenactment cuts through the *Four Quartets* and is their subject and technique, as the dancer from Yeats embodies the concord of form and content, of actor and action. Many motives are late revealed: the nostalgia for childhood bliss; adolescent rebellion against home's constraints; the longing for transcendent knowledge; the hope of poetic success; the trials of love; the calamities of history; the desire to restore ancestral orders; the dream of new ships, of a language that could carry exploring old men past Byzantium's glitter to a justified paradise. The "exercise of virtue," in retrospect, had also been an evasion of self-knowledge in a waste of ill-conceived opinions "done to others' harm." Eliot carries Dante's method to its logical conclusion, consigns himself to hell, purgatory, and judgment. The "refining fire" now burning with the announcements of pentecostal flames is a text and a state of the soul: it is a processing of identity through other corrective voices, an intertextual conflagration wherein "you must move in measure, like a dancer." If one reads the scene as, among other things, an interior agon between recurrent self-images, then it epitomizes what Lawrence Lipking isolates as a major purpose of *Four Quartets*: to self-consciously reread the entirety of Eliot's career in poetry, selecting and shaping its fragments into some version of that epic unity or coherent view of life that he believed distinguished great poets from mere versifiers.

The poet and the man measure steps among the living and the dead, choreograph a pattern of connections, displacements, and repositionings. There are no intermissions for the dancer of endless humility, no resting on the ground or in the heavens. This dancer's pained ecstasy is performed in the theater of repetition. Knowledge of self and other comes through representation, as a reading of the dance of estrangements and homecomings, their motives, virtues, and ends. The poet begins and ends on that estranging stage: "I cannot find any alternative for either 'enchantment' or 're-enactment' which does not either lose or alter meaning. 'Re-enacting' is weak as a substantive; and I want to preserve the association of 'enact'—to take the part of oneself on a stage for oneself as the audience." So goes the drama of "impersonality."

With the end of the ghost's speech, the curtain falls on this scene of instruction, while it rises on that of the encompassing poem itself. The theater that is the poem starts up; the reader in the audience watches as the section closes at dawn and reenacts in its ending the beginning of Hamlet.

The day was breaking. In the disfigured street
He left me, with a kind of valediction,
And faded on the blowing of the horn.

Eliot rejected an editorial suggestion by Hayward concerning these lines on the grounds that it would "mean my losing the allusion to Hamlet's ghost," the specter he had not even mentioned in his early essay on the play. The allusion does more than just effect a neat symmetry between the all-clear siren and the crowing of the cock that dismissed Hamlet's father "like a guilty thing / Upon a fearful summons." That moment comes at the beginning of the tragedy, this at the end. The conflation and inversion help to situate this part of the poem as a kind of prologue to what is possible. It holds open the possibility of reversing the tragic course of Shakespeare's play, in which the son is doomed by the return of the dead and the callousness of the living. The horn comes after the destructive night, leaving us in a yet "uncertain hour" to face the days this colloquy has prepared for. The play, the reenactment of these words, is left in the audience-reader's hands. The street has been "disfigured" as well as transfigured. The puns on the former term include ruination, depopulation, and the confusion of destruction. But on this literary street, disfiguration also means the compounding of various poetic "figures" into this "dead master." Language has disfigured experience and made a strange place accessible. Figures are "breaking," sounding a farewell to past identities.

There is "a kind of valediction" at the end of certain speech, a diction of breakings and dawnings that also bids a reverent good-bye to what it disfigures. This valediction forbids mourning, for this morning sees the patterned reconciliation of double parts. The allusion to Donne's poem fits the implication of distance reserved in measurement. Donne and his lady assume their double parts: "If they be two, they are two so / As stiff twin compasses are two." The precision of Donne's conceit and the faith he has in his centering love bring him expertly home.

> And though it in the center sit,
>   Yet when the other far doth roam,
> It leans and hearkens after it,
>   And grows erect, as that comes home.
> Such wilt thou be to me, who must
>   Like th'other foot, obliquely run;
> Thy firmness makes my circle just,
>   And makes me end where I begun.

The circle, so often invoked in discussions of the *Quartets*, appears at first to manage this section of "Little Gidding." It moves from the "uncertain hour before morning" through the "intersection time" and back to the breaking of day. The firmness of the style and the ghost's poetically constructed authority make Eliot's circle "just," as it does justice to each of the many parts played by tradition and the individual talent. Where he ends, with the lessons of the past, is where he sat down to write this "imitation" of Dante. Yet, the foot of Eliot's compass is a ghost, a shadowy figure obliquely running. His ending beginning is a breaking of the circle. The blowing of the horn trumpets the fading of even a ghostly center, leaving poet and reader at the recurrent dawning of the ending. Donne's poem recollects reunion in a metaphor of circumscription; Eliot's poem repeats Donne's and breaks it into reinscriptions that can never be exactly measured.

Breaking occurs in repetition, as repetition disfigures what it represents. Thus, in the light of the eclipse, dawn breaks on the "present," and memory finds its vocation.

> This is the use of memory:
> For liberation—not less of love but expanding
> Of love beyond desire, and so liberation
> From the future as well as the past.
>
> (LG, III)

Eliot goes on to reject the notion of memory as nostalgic recollection and to repudiate thinking of the future as if it were simply perpetuation or recovery.

> History may be servitude,
> History may be freedom. See, now they vanish,
> The faces and places, with the self which, as it could, loved them,
> To become renewed, transfigured, in another pattern.
>
> (LG, III)

The same interplay of recollection and repetition pertains to "history." The weight of historical inheritance lightens when "servitude" to the past becomes the "freedom" of transfiguration/disfiguration. The end of Western history, here in England and always, ceases to be a privileged, unique catastrophe. It, too, dismally repeats and must be made the occasion of a renewal sprung from disillusion. Because "history is a pattern / Of timeless moments," Eliot believes that "A people without history / Is not redeemed from time" by forgetfulness or resignation to the Same (LG, V). The timelessness of ghostly moments and their passions depends on the purpose of the historical memory. Condemned to repeat history in interpretation, humanity at least has the option of refusing to repeat it in action. Wars are revenge tragedies, directed at another whose conquest offers the delusion of purgation. Against this, Eliot counsels relinquishment, though not appeasement.

Eliot supports the war against fascism. What he questions, most pointedly in "The Idea of a Christian Society," is the "validity of a civilisation" centered on the economic imperative; a civilization deluded by the promise of recuperated investments, living as if fresh profits could erase the traces of human loss and degradation without accounting for their wastes. Eliot wondered if the combatants were dissimilar only in the degree to which they would brutalize and exploit life for political power and economic gain. Through an odd lens compounded of Marx and Christ, which often yielded strange visions, Eliot interrogated that "organization of society on the principle of private profit, as well as public destruction" reigning throughout the West, connecting the Allies and Axis in a single pattern. On this, that the root causes of the war were economic and spiritual, Pound and Eliot largely agreed. The fires of the war present an opportunity for reexamining the servitude to ruling ideologies perpetuated by corrupt desires and bad memories. Time will reduce all to vanity; freedom may be facilitated by bidding farewell to them, allowing them to vanish in the revision of humility. The war provides the "objective correlative" of the meditation that is "Little Gidding." How we are to recover from it, how its irreparable losses are to be fit into a progressive, profitable philosophical economy, poetry cannot say without disfiguring and disillusioning the partisans on every side.

Incarnating breakage, the war repeats the pattern Eliot finds in memory and literature. In fact, the poems of the *Quartets* link their subjects and levels of discourse in a general philosophical argument about the economy of waste and enrichments, in which the war is but another, if terrifying, example. In section 5 of "Little Gidding" the argument moves from the particular manifestation of the war to the general reflection on loss, value, and the aberrant economy they figure when covenants of measurement are suspended. Adjusted to the surprises at play in remembrance, the poem economically transfigures its own recollections of itself: "What we call the beginning is often the end / And to make an end is to make a beginning. / The end is where we start from." Previously we had started from "home." Home ends now; our being at home in the poem is ending. We shall soon start up from the text, go home, begin again, and find home transfigured as this text produces a different text from the one we had initially figured. The "home" we come to is a process of understanding characterized by its identification with the structure of language.

> And every phrase
> And every sentence that is right (where every word is at home,
> Taking its place to support the others,
> The word neither diffident nor ostentatious,
> An easy commerce of the old and the new,
> The common word exact without vulgarity,
> The formal word precise but not pedantic,
> The complete consort dancing together)
> Every phrase and every sentence is an end and a beginning,
> Every poem an epitaph.
>
> (LG, V)

The ideal "commerce" set off in parentheses might be assimilated to a theology of poetic formalism or unanxious influence were it not equally asserted that every poem is "an epitaph." The poem, or any utterance, elegizes. It commemorates loss, marking the grave of that passionate moment language can only approach belatedly in a representation. And it marks its own grave, too, dies onto the page: "And any action / Is a step to the block, to the fire, down the sea's throat / Or to an illegible stone: and that is where we start." We are at home with illegible stones, in the graveyard/library of tumbled expressions, "dancing together" with the dead.

The act of writing violates the calm of supposed securities, marks the whiteness of the page and moment with a darkness into which we read. Reading starts with the illegible, and the illegible is its end. Reading repeats the act of disfiguring/transfiguring as it produces yet another pattern of language: every interpretation an epitaph. That pattern in turn appears illegible to the future that castrates, murders, loves, and resurrects it. Inscriptions, like the entombed Madeline Usher, break from their crypts with meanings beyond the figured purpose, called from their graves by their living literary lovers. Writing and reading supplement each other's destructive acts, die into each other's embrace, are each other's ghostly double, and reproduce life in their narrative. The process is memory's, too, and also conditions the formation of knowledge about identity, time, and being: "We are born with the dead." The poem will itself die and in its final stanza be born with the dying lines gathered up and returned from their previous incarnations. These last lines of the *Quartets* create an Eliotic palimpsest, its form of repetition perfectly tuned to the theme of a renewal in illegibility, an ecstatic unknowing of past versions. Unceasing exploration arrives "where we started" and knows "the place for the first time" as an epitaph, thus a liberation. To know "Through the unknown, remembered gate" is to write/remember the place out of place, to be in a present place and know it as the displacement of where we have been. What was remembered was unknown, and it is known now by a repetition that occurs "When the last of earth left to discover / Is that which was the beginning." By repeating his American beginnings ("the source of the longest river / The voice of the hidden waterfall / And the children in the apple-tree"), the poet unknows them. They are severed from enchainment to past meaning or future deliverance and are made sights of rediscovery. They were

> Not known, because not looked for
> But heard, half-heard, in the stillness
> Between two waves of the sea.

These moments, "Quick now, here, now, always—" signify the evanescent and ungraspable sensations of the moment, always flickering just before language arrives to take them home and make them known. Known, like woman to this imagination, they fall. The imagination may figure for us, remembering, the idea of a virgin present "Between two waves of the sea," like Aphrodite sprung from the breakers of past and future. In the wake of this breaking is not an absence, but the fully resounding language of ghostly compounds, voicing real beauties.

Understanding this loss and gain, readying conservation for metamorphosis into projection, the imagination, compounded of emotion and intellect, suffers a sea change to "A condition of complete simplicity / (Costing not less than everything)." Possessed by way of dispossession, the poet treasures remembered beauties as potential repetitions, recurrences exceeding the taxonomy of living and dead, same and different—and in that excess known for the first time. These categories break, in literature as in life, when the covenant of identity and abstraction is distracted, revolved as in Dante's final canto of the *Paradiso* by the loving will that explores the illegible details of passionate moments. The writing of exploration recovers by awakening/dying into the eternity of transfiguring, disillusioning dawns. An altered sense is given to Emerson's prophetic assertion at the beginning of *Nature* that "the sun shines to-day also." Night and day forever interpenetrating, the divine sun always a ghost on the horizon, losses are tossed up, and memories supplied that they may burn to light the presence of day.

> And all shall be well and
> All manner of thing shall be well
> When the tongues of flame are in-folded
> Into the crowned knot of fire
> And the fire and the rose are one.

Eliot ends reenvisioning Dante's paradisial end, recalling the ingathering of "substances and accidents and their relations" that are "bound by love in one single volume." Disfigured by Eliot, the vision incorporates an image of passionate and destructive change in the connotations now carried by flame and fire. This fire combines the actions of disintegration and revision in producing its transfigurations of the past. The flames of poetic tongues gather, laced rather than fused, in a knot that reserves their individual strands as they are tied together in a singular incendiary device. The "crowned knot of fire" stands for the torchlight that is tradition, the intersection world, the suspended timing of texts and repetitions burning to illuminate the darkness they discover at beginning and end. A dazzling metaphor, the fiery knot lights the paths of literature and consciousness, consuming the fuels of desire. So conceived and put to the torch, "the fire and the rose are one." The rose of perfection, recollection, and order is also "in-folded" in the erotic and literary fire, thus uniting the hue of natural passion with the color of the tongues of flame to form a final figure for personal and poetic history.

The rose garden is on fire. The desire for unity, consummation, bliss, the eternal recurrence of the Same, undergoes its last askesis. Polysemous, the emblem of the rose unites nature's Eros with poetry's theology in order to refine the longings and delusions of both. As a knot of fire, the rose becomes an eternal flame of enlightened disillusionment, a process of love that gains energy from its losses of identity and grows strong in the repetition of other times it heatedly ingathers. Love, as the overcoming of self-consciousness and the repetition of an ancient pattern in modern figures, renews itself just as the poem is renewed by entwining itself with its precursors. Purged of its illusions, the rose dances in the "tongues of flame" that repeat and inspire it, re-marking the measures of poetry and love.

Chronology

1670	Andrew Eliot, T.S. Eliot's ancestor, emigrated from East Coker, Somerset, to settle in Massachusetts.
1834	Rev. William Greenleaf Eliot (Unitarian), T.S. Eliot's grandfather, settled in St. Louis, Missouri.
1888	Thomas Stearns Eliot born September 26, in St. Louis. Youngest of seven children born to Henry Ware Eliot and Charlotte Eliot (née Stearns).
1906–10	Undergraduate at Harvard. Discovered the Symbolists and Laforgue. An editor of the *Harvard Advocate*, a literary magazine.
1910–11	Studied in Paris at the Sorbonne. Visited Germany. Wrote "Preludes," "Prufrock," "Portrait of a Lady," "Rhapsody on a Windy Night" and "La Figlia che Piange," 1910–12.
1911–14	Graduate student in philosophy at Harvard. Began dissertation on the philosophy of F.H. Bradley.
1914	Study at the University of Marburg, Germany, cut off by war. Residence at Merton College, Oxford. Met Ezra Pound.
1915–16	"Prufrock" published in *Poetry*, in Chicago, and in *Blast*, in England, 1915. Teaching and reviewing in London. Completed Bradley thesis. Married to Vivien Haigh-Wood, 1915.
1917–19	Employee of Lloyd's Bank. Assistant Editor of *The Egoist*, 1917–19. *Prufrock and Other Observations*, 1917. "Tradition and the Individual Talent," 1919.
1920	*Poems* and *The Sacred Wood*. Began *The Waste Land*.
1922	Editor of *The Criterion*, until its closure in 1939. Dial Award for *The Waste Land*.
1924	"Four Elizabethan Dramatists."
1925	*The Hollow Men* and *Poems, 1909–25*. Joined Faber & Gwyer, later Faber & Faber, publishers.
1926	Two "Fragments" (of *Sweeney Agonistes*).
1927–31	Became a member of the Church of England and a British citizen, 1927. *Ariel Poems*, 1927–31. *For Lancelot Andrewes*, 1928. *Ash-Wednesday*, 1930. *Coriolan*, 1931. *Thoughts After Lambeth*, 1931.

1932–33   First visit to America since 1914. Delivered Charles Eliot Norton Lectures at Harvard (published as *The Use of Poetry and the Use of Criticism*, 1933), and the Page-Barbour Lectures at the University of Virginia (published as *After Strange Gods—A Primer of Modern Heresy*, 1934). *Selected Essays*. Break-up of first marriage.

1934   *The Rock*.

1935–36   *Murder in the Cathedral. Collected Poems, 1909–35*, including "Burnt Norton," 1936.

1939   Delivered the Cambridge Lectures, published as *The Idea of a Christian Society. The Family Reunion*.

1940–44   *Four Quartets*, 1943. Part time fire-watcher, 1940–41. "What is a Classic?," 1944.

1945   Lectured in Washington. Visited Ezra Pound at St. Elizabeth's Hospital. Shared an apartment in London with John Hayward until 1957.

1947   Honorary degree from Harvard. Death of first wife, after long illness.

1948   Awarded the Order of Merit and the Nobel Prize for Literature. *Notes Toward a Definition of Culture*.

1950   *The Cocktail Party*.

1951   Suffered a mild heart attack. In poor health thereafter.

1954–55   Awarded the Hanseatic Goethe Prize, 1954. *The Confidential Clerk*.

1956   Lectured in Minneapolis on "The Frontiers of Criticism."

1957   *On Poetry and Poets*. Married Valerie Fletcher, his personal secretary.

1959   *The Elder Statesman*.

1961   Lectured at Leeds, published as "To Criticize the Critic."

1962–63   Seriously ill in London. Visited New York with Valerie Eliot, 1963.

1965   Died in London, January 4.

Contributors

HAROLD BLOOM, editor of the Chelsea House Modern Critical Views series, is Sterling Professor of the Humanities at Yale University. His books include *Yeats*, *The Anxiety of Influence*, and the forthcoming *Freud: Transference and Authority*. He is the general editor of the Chelsea House Library of Literary Criticism.

DENIS DONOGHUE is Henry James Professor of English and American Literature at New York University. His books include *The Third Voice*, *The Sovereign Ghost* and *Ferocious Alphabets*.

RICHARD ELLMANN, perhaps the leading literary biographer of our time, is Professor of English at Emory University, and formerly Goldsmiths Professor at Oxford. His major works include biographies of Yeats and Joyce, and a widely awaited forthcoming life of Oscar Wilde.

NORTHROP FRYE, formerly University Professor of the University of Toronto, is regarded by the editor of this volume as the foremost literary critic since Ruskin and Pater. He wrote *Fearful Symmetry*, still the best study of William Blake, and *Anatomy of Criticism*, among many other works.

MICHAEL GOLDMAN, Professor of English at Princeton, has written on Shakespeare and on modern drama.

LYNDALL GORDON can be said to be Eliot's most sensitive biographical critic to date. She is lecturer in English at Oxford University.

GREGORY JAY teaches English at the University of Alabama. He has written extensively upon contemporary criticism.

HUGH KENNER teaches at Johns Hopkins University. He is the canonical critic of Anglo-American literary "modernism," widely admired for his studies of Joyce, Eliot, Pound and Wyndham Lewis.

RUTH NEVO, South African by birth, is Professor of English at the Hebrew University in Jerusalem, Israel. She is greatly esteemed for her critical writing on Shakespeare and on seventeenth century literature. Her principal works include *Tragic Form in Shakespeare* and *The Dial of Virtue*.

JAMES OLNEY is Professor of English at Louisiana State University, where he edits the *Southern Review*. Besides his *Metaphors of Self: The Meaning of Autobiography*, he has edited *Autobiography: Essays Theoretical and Critical*.

Bibliography

Auden, W.H. *The Dyer's Hand*. New York: Random House, 1962.

Bergonzi, Bernard. *T.S. Eliot*. New York: Collier Books, 1972.

Blackmur, R.P. *Anni Mirabiles: 1921–1925*. Washington, D.C.: The Library of Congress, 1956.

Brooks, Cleanth. *Modern Poetry and the Tradition*. Chapel Hill: University of North Carolina Press, 1939.

Drew, Elizabeth. *T.S. Eliot: The Design of His Poetry*. New York: Scribner's, 1949.

Eliot, Valerie. *The Waste Land: A Facsimile and Transcript*. New York: Harcourt Brace Jovanovich, 1971.

Frye, Northrop. *T.S. Eliot*. New York: Grove, 1963.

Gallup, Donald. *T.S. Eliot: A Bibliography*. New York: Harcourt Brace Jovanovich, 1953. Revised edition 1969.

Gardner, Helen. *The Art of T.S. Eliot*. New York: Dutton, 1959.

Gordon, Lyndall. *Eliot's Early Years*. Oxford and New York: Oxford University Press, 1977.

Grant, Michael, ed. *T.S. Eliot: The Critical Heritage*. London: Routledge & Kegan Paul Ltd., 1982. 2 vols.

Jay, Gregory S. *T.S. Eliot and the Poetics of Literary History*. Baton Rouge: Louisiana State University Press, 1983.

Kenner, Hugh. *The Invisible Poet: T.S. Eliot*. New York: Harcourt Brace Jovanovich, 1969.

———, ed. *T.S. Eliot: A Collection of Critical Essays*. New Jersey: Prentice-Hall, 1962.

Kermode, Frank, ed. *Selected Prose of T.S. Eliot*. New York: Harcourt Brace Jovanovich, 1975.

Kojecký, Roger. *T.S. Eliot's Social Criticism*. New York: Farrar, Strauss & Giroux, 1972.

Leavis, F.R. "T.S. Eliot." In *New Bearings in English Poetry*. 2nd ed. Ann Arbor: University of Michigan Press, 1960.

Litz, A. Walton. "'That Strange Abstraction: Nature': T.S. Eliot's Victorian Inheritance," in U.C. Knoepflmacher and G.B. Tennyson, eds., *Nature and the Victorian Imagination*. Berkeley: University of California Press, 1977.

———, ed. *Eliot in His Time*. Princeton: Princeton University Press, 1973.

Lucy, Sean. *T.S. Eliot and the Idea of Tradition*. London: Cohen & West, 1960.

Margolis, John D. *T.S. Eliot's Intellectual Development*. Chicago: University of Chicago Press, 1972.

Martin, Graham, ed. *Eliot in Perspective: A Symposium*. New York: Humanities, 1970.

Matthiessen, F.O. *The Achievement of T.S. Eliot.* 3rd ed. New York: Oxford University Press, 1958.

Moody, A.L. *Thomas Stearns Eliot, Poet.* Cambridge: Harvard University Press, 1981.

Olney, James. *Metaphors of Self: The Meaning of Autobiography.* Princeton: Princeton University Press, 1972.

Rajan, B., ed. *T.S. Eliot: A Study of His Writings by Several Hands.* London: Dobson, 1947.

Richards, I.A. *Poetries and Sciences.* New York: Norton, 1970.

Robbins, R.H. *The T.S. Eliot Myth.* New York: Schuman, 1951.

Schneider, Elizabeth. *T.S. Eliot: The Pattern in the Carpet.* Berkeley: University of California Press, 1975.

Scofield, Martin. "T.S. Eliot's Images of Love." *Critical Quarterly* 18 (Autumn 1976): 5–26.

Serio, John N. "Landscape and Voice in T.S. Eliot's Poetry." *Centennial Review* (Winter 1982): 33–50.

Smith, Grover. *T.S. Eliot's Poetry and Plays.* Chicago: University of Chicago Press, 1974.

Spender, Stephen. *T.S. Eliot.* New York: Penguin Books, 1975.

Stead, C.K. *The New Poetic.* London: Hutchinson, 1964.

Tate, Allen, ed. *T.S. Eliot: The Man and His Work.* London: Chatto & Windus, 1967.

Unger, Leonard. *T.S. Eliot: Moments and Patterns.* Minneapolis: University of Minnesota Press, 1967.

———, ed. *T.S. Eliot: A Selected Critique.* New York: Holt, Rinehart & Winston, Inc., 1948.

Williamson, George. *A Reader's Guide to T.S. Eliot.* New York: Noonday Press, 1957.

Wilson, Edmund. *Axel's Castle.* New York: Scribner's, 1931.

Acknowledgments

"Ash-Wednesday" by Hugh Kenner from *The Invisible Poet: T.S. Eliot* by Hugh Kenner, copyright © 1959 by Hugh Kenner. Reprinted by permission of McDowell, Obolensky, Inc.

"Antique Drum" by Northrop Frye from *T.S. Eliot* by Northrop Frye, copyright © 1963 by Northrop Frye. Reprinted by permission of University of Chicago Press.

"Four Quartets: 'folded in a single party'" by James Olney from *Metaphors of Self: The Meaning of Autobiography* by James Olney, copyright © 1972 by Princeton University Press. Reprinted by permission.

"Fear in the Way: The Design of Eliot's Drama" by Michael Goldman from *Eliot in His Time* edited by A. Walton Litz, copyright © 1973 by Princeton University Press. Reprinted by permission.

"Prometheus in Straits: Lawrence and Eliot" by Denis Donoghue from *Thieves of Fire* by Denis Donoghue, copyright © 1973 by Denis Donoghue. Reprinted by permission of Oxford University Press.

"The First Waste Land" by Richard Ellmann from *Eliot in His Time* edited by A. Walton Litz, copyright © 1973 by Princeton University Press. Reprinted by permission.

"Conversion" by Lyndall Gordon from *Eliot's Early Years* by Lyndall Gordon, copyright © 1977 by Oxford University Press. Reprinted by permission.

"*The Waste Land*: Ur-Text of Deconstruction" by Ruth Nevo from *New Literary History*, Volume XIII, Spring 1982, no. 3, copyright © 1982 by *New Literary History*. Reprinted by permission.

"Ghosts and Roses" by Gregory S. Jay from *T.S. Eliot and the Poetics of Literary History* by Gregory S. Jay, copyright © 1983 by Louisiana State University Press. Reprinted by permission.

Index